WE
ABOVE
ME

WE
ABOVE
ME

UNDERSTANDING THE BIBLICAL LINK BETWEEN
LOVE AND NEEDS FOR A UNIFIED MARRIAGE

ERIC & CHERI WINTERTON

The authors are grateful to all the pastors, past and present, of Rosedale Baptist Church led by the Senior Pastor, Dr. Scott Tewell for their Godly wisdom, prayers, encouragement, and support throughout this entire process.

First edition: October 2018

ISBN 978-1-7326833-3-4

The events and conversations in this book have been written to the best of the author's ability, although some names and details have been changed to improve continuity and/or protect the privacy of individuals.

All scripture quotations are from the King James Version

Illustrations copyright © 2018 by Eric and Cheri Winterton

Forward by: Dr. Scott Tewell

Find out more about Eric & Cheri Winterton at www.wintertonstory.com

It is with great parental love that we dedicate this book to our boys,
Matthew, A.J., and Ryan.
If you keep your focus on God, your life will be blessed.

TABLE OF CONTENTS

FOREWORD

The book you are about to read should be read with urgency. As a pastor, I feel this urgency deeply for two reasons. First, I have become aware of hurting people all around me struggling in the area of marriage. They are resentful, angry, brokenhearted, and, most sadly, without hope. Even as Christians, we have bought into society's cheap version of the husband and wife relationship. For most of society, their view of marriage is low. As a result, marriages are failing.

Secondly, I feel an urgency for you to read this book because of the importance God has placed on marriage. Marriage isn't just a way for us to have happiness, security, and a mutual meeting of needs. Marriage is the beautiful picture that God has chosen to display His covenant with man. It's a supernatural, awe-inspiring, logic-defying pact that supersedes our sin and our selfishness and stands the test of time.

Eric and Cheri Winterton write from both of these places.

Eric and Cheri's first marriages were to people who believed in Christ but didn't practice Christ's principles for marriage. There was no biblical application of the grace and love they'd experienced in salvation played out in marriage. Marriage was compartmentalized, separate, and unconnected.

And both of their marriages failed.

Statistics show that a second marriage is even more likely to fail than a first. There was no reason to believe that this second marriage would be any better than their first ones, that it would end any differently. The odds were not good.

But something happened in Eric and Cheri's hearts between that first marriage and the second one. This second marriage was intentionally built upon the principles of God's Word about Christ-honoring marriages. They carefully studied, meditated, and prayed over Scripture to allow the Holy Spirit to change their view of marriage. It needed rebuilding from the ground up.

God's view of marriage is vastly different and more wonderful than anything we can imagine. And we can't know this type of marriage apart from God; He has to be the one to teach it to us through His Word.

This book presents you with that opportunity. Will you walk through Scripture with the Wintertons and ask the Author of marriage to teach you His ways? Will you challenge your ideas of marriage and question your commitment? This beautiful, messy, difficult relationship called marriage is unlike any other, but it's the one human relationship God chose to glorify Himself through as a picture of Christ and the church. Understanding marriage from God's perspective gives a deeper, multi-prismatic picture of the gospel.

Not only will this book walk you through the biblical view of marriage from a philosophical standpoint but it will also take those ideas and outline very practical steps to living out God's plan for your marriage each day. Revolutionary ideas are boiled down to the very practical through homework, questions for conversation, and the nuts and bolts of interactions that will help you implement what you've learned as you reflect that beautiful gospel message through your marriage.

The ideas in this book are tried and true. Following the transformation in their own lives, the Wintertons were asked to share what they had learned in small group settings designed for couples facing the unique challenges of second marriages and blended families. It quickly became apparent that this study of the biblical view of marriage would be beneficial to an even wider audience of couples. The class grew in number and, more importantly, in spirit as hearts were changed, paths were altered, and relationships were healed.

The material you will study here has been used for counseling and mentoring couples in crises. Over and over, we've seen dramatic results that can only be explained by the power of the Word of God to change lives when nothing else can.

Maybe you are one of those in crisis, frustrated and without hope. Perhaps you're simply disappointed in your marriage and wonder if it can ever be better than it is right now. Maybe you don't have anyone to confide in and wonder if others have walked this path as well.

Keep reading. I have seen the biblical principles explained in these pages play out in the flesh-and-bone marriage of one of the strongest families we have in our church. There is hope. Your marriage can be healed. Walk with Eric and Cheri through these pages, and experience the change you've longed for.

Sincerely,
Dr. Scott Tewell
Senior Pastor
Rosedale Baptist Church

PROLOGUE

According to the last census, completed in 2010, only 40.5% of Americans were married at that time. This is a large decline from the 84% of people that were married at the time of the 1970 census. Part of this statistic is due to people getting married at older ages or choosing to cohabitate in lieu of marriage. Another main driver is that divorce rates have significantly increased over the past 40 years. The census also shows that many people have chosen to cohabit rather than get married and that just under 50% of all first marriages lasted more than 20 years. What

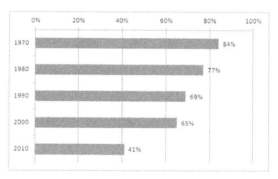

Figure 1 - A Smaller Share of Adults Are Married (% Currently Married)

has been going on in America over the past 40 decades? All of this data points to the fact that most people have given up on marriage. They are ill-equipped to handle a life-long commitment to marriage because they don't understand what marriage means anymore. Current culture seems to embrace the idea of living together before marriage; however, the census shows that people that do so are significantly more likely to end up divorced. People that had premarital births also were at an increased risk of divorce. This book was written as a guide to people that want to understand what it means to be in a healthy marriage and want to know the secrets to *being* the right person, *finding* the right person, and *staying* happily married to that person until death do them part.

If you are thinking of marriage but have doubts about the marriage lasting, my wife and I are in a unique position to tell you that we have traveled down both roads ahead of you: We have done marriage the wrong way and the right way. I personally was one of those divorce statistics. I have fathered not one but two kids out of wedlock from two different mothers. I lived with both of them, I married one of them, and the total combined time spent living with these women was fewer than five years. Living with these women was good initially, but within a year, our lives turned into a constant struggle. It seemed like one good day would be just enough to get me through an entire week of difficulty. I had constant stress, was rarely happy, and never had peace.

Cheri was married for almost 10 years and had one son with her ex-husband. Although they both believed in God, got married in the church, and went to "premarital classes," neither one of them had a personal relationship with God. Within a year of being married, evidence was clear that they only thought of themselves and what they could get out of the marriage. Cheri admits that they had a lonely, self-centered marriage.

Cheri and I were married on New Year's Day in 2005. There is no better time than the first day of a new year to start a NEW BEGINNING! Cheri's son walked her down the aisle and stood as her "man of honor." My two boys were my best man and ring bearer. It was the joining of two families, and the five of us were so excited to become one blended family.

Although we have had our share of difficulties, the days of joy, peace, and happiness have outshined any issues we have ever faced. In fact, I love my wife more now than I did the day we met. What changed? Why did this second marriage succeed and my first two serious relationships fail? There are many reasons, and I will cover those in this book in depth, but mostly I changed through a relationship with Jesus Christ. I found peace, joy, and happiness that has grown in proportion to the relationship I have with Christ. The stronger my walk, the more I study, memorize, and meditate on the Word of God and the better my marriage has become. My wife also has a heart for the Lord, and as we both have drawn closer to God, we have drawn closer together.

This book will reveal the things that you must do to make a marriage work successfully and what you need to avoid doing to prevent your marriage from falling apart. According to an August 2013 survey done by Institute for Divorce Financial Analysts,[1] these are the top three reasons for divorce:

- Incompatibility (43%)
- Infidelity (28%)
- Financial issues (22%)

This book will focus on these three topics to ensure that you are compatible with your mate, to protect you from infidelity, and to teach you how to properly handle your money as a couple. How wonderful would it be to enter into marriage knowing that you are equipped with the knowledge and tools you need to protect your marriage from 93% of the problems that can cause divorce? To go to the altar with confidence, not just in your heart but in your head, because you know both the privilege and responsibilities of a married couple? It is our sincere hope that this book will help you to understand the biblical link between love and needs that will make your marriage more unified. We have included lots of tools that you can use to avoid the mistakes Cheri and I made to help your only marriage be like the one Cheri and I have today. May this book bring a revival to the institution of marriage today in America.

Disclaimer: There are many testimonies throughout this book. All of them are absolutely true; however, some details may be omitted and the story modified to improve continuity and protect the people beyond our immediate family. Our intention is not to

---

1 https://www.prweb.com/releases/2013/8/prweb10980724.htm

cast anyone in a negative light. The point is to show the contrast between our lives without God in them and how much better life is when we are unified with God and with each other.

1

WHAT IS LOVE?

I'm 10 years old, and I hop out of bed on a Saturday morning excited to watch the Saturday morning cartoons. I run down the hall toward the living room ready to leap on the sofa, only to be stopped in my tracks. My mom is sitting with my older brother, both of them with tears streaming down their faces. She waves me over. Suddenly Saturday morning cartoons are not that important any longer. *What is going on?* I wonder. *Did someone die? Or maybe she is just sad because Dad has been traveling a lot lately. Now that I think about it, I can't remember the last time my dad was home more than he was on the road. He is taking business trips a lot lately.* I crawl up on her lap and look my mother in the face. She tells me my dad is not coming back from his business trip. He is moving out. They are getting a divorce. The family is dissolved. Ruined. Everyone is crying. Suddenly I do feel like someone died. Maybe a little of all of us died that day.

On another Saturday morning, hundreds of miles away, a young girl named Cheri wakes up to the sounds of plates clinking, the smell of coffee brewing, and bacon sizzling. She walks down the steps and into the kitchen, where all the noise and yummy smells are coming from. There she sees her mom at the stove making breakfast and her dad at the head of the table, reading the local paper and sipping his coffee. Before she makes her presence known, she just watches them. Mom is chatting about the day's plans, and Dad is glancing over his paper, hanging on her every word, with just the slightest smile on his face. He puts down his coffee and paper, walks over to her mother, and hugs her from behind. Mom spins around and squeezes him tight. It's at that moment that they notice their daughter standing there. She runs to them, her dad picks her up, and the three of them hug. Just then her three older sisters barge in on their moment, and the kitchen is now aflutter with chatter and activity. A happy, joyful family.

What leads one family to come together only to be destroyed?

Why is another family so happy?

What is the difference between a loving Christian family and a worldly family?

The Bible has the answers. It starts with each individual in the family. It starts with you and your mindset toward your family and toward life. The biblical truths in this book will not only help your family but will help <u>every</u> relationship you have, including the one you have (or will have) with Jesus Christ.

WHAT IS LOVE?

To understand love and marriage as defined by the Bible, we need to start by diving into the biblical truth about love. There are many Bible passages that discuss love, and even in the original Greek language, there are at least three words that all mean love: eros, philia, and agape. Is it any wonder the world we live in today is confused by the word love? You may hear people say, "I love pizza," or "I love football," and then they will say the words "I love you" to someone. If you ask them to define love, they stutter and stumble, and no two definitions are ever the same. If you are anything like me, you may be confused too. That is, until I studied the Word of God, the Bible.

In the past, I was confused about what love was. I didn't know God, I didn't know God's Word, and therefore I didn't know love. Unfortunately, a great many people today are in the same boat.

1 John 4:8 – He that loveth not knoweth not God; for God is love.

I've been married twice in my life. The first time was without God, and it lasted 17 months. My marriage with God in it has lasted 13 years and has gotten stronger each and every year. My first marriage was full of despair, pain, and two selfish people who didn't know God and therefore didn't know how to treat one another. Those 17 months felt like forever! My second marriage, my godly marriage, my marriage to a godly woman, is so full of positive memories that it seems like it was just yesterday when we exchanged vows with one another. Time has flown! We have so many happy moments. We know God on a personal level, and the closer to Him we draw, the closer to one another we get.

As you can see in this graphic, the closer you and your spouse move toward God, the closer you are to each other. Coincidence? Not at all. God is love, and the more you understand Him, the more you will understand love and the better able you will be to give that love to others.

Three Kinds of Love

The word love can be translated from three different Greek words. Each word means something completely different. Let's explore the different meanings of love. Simply put, they mean the following:

- Eros – romance
- Philia – friendship
- Agape – charity

Eros

Eros is physical love. It is where we get the root of the word erotic. When you admire someone's physical features, athletic figure, cute face, etc., that is eros love. Eros love is when you are physically attracted to another person.

Philia

Philia is friendship. The name Philadelphia came from philia and is often referred to as the city of brotherly love. Philia love is when you have things in common with someone. In other words, you are attracted to people that think like you do and like the same things you do. Do you agree on politics, religion, movies, food, sports, entertainment, or other interests? This commonality among different people also creates an attraction to another person. You enjoy being around those people who agree with you. The more you have in common, the more philia love you have with people.

Agape

Finally, we have agape, which translates into the English word "charity." What is charity? I've looked at several definitions that don't do this word nearly enough justice. The way most people think of it, charity is giving to the poor or needy. While this is a good example of charity, it still doesn't completely explain the word. Here is my definition:

4

> Charity – The giving of a product or services to <u>meet the needs</u> of another person <u>without expectation</u> of payment

You aren't charitable if you expect someone to earn what you are giving them. If I give canned goods to a homeless shelter, I don't expect the homeless person to come wash my car or mow my lawn, right? If I did that, it wouldn't be charity. The homeless person would be earning the canned goods. It's not a gift if it's earned. One key aspect of charity is to give without expecting anything in return.

The second aspect of the definition is to make sure that the product or service is meeting a need. If I donate an Xbox video game to a homeless shelter, that really doesn't help meet the needs of the hungry or someone who doesn't have a home. In order to be charitable, it must meet a need. Agape love is meeting the needs of another person by providing a product or service without expecting anything in return. The two important elements of charity/love/agape are that it requires giving without expectation of payment (a gift) and that it must meet a need for the person it is intended for.

The agape love definition clearly fits the context of 1 John 4:8, where God describes himself. This definition also fits the context of John 3:16:

> *For God so loved the world, that he <u>gave</u> his <u>only begotten Son</u>, that whosoever believeth in him shall not perish, but have <u>everlasting life</u>.*

God "gave." He offered us something of value, not expecting us to pay him back. That is why we can't earn our way into heaven (Eph. 2:8–9). What was the gift? "His only begotten son." What need did that gift meet in us (the world)? "Everlasting life". Now, that is a gift worth receiving.

There is a stark contrast among the different types of love. Eros and philia are both an attraction to someone, a feeling; they are both focused on what you can get from someone you are attracted to. Compare that to agape love, where there is no attraction but rather a responsibility; it is you giving, not getting. Eros and philia are attractions based on what you *get* out of the other person as opposed to what you can *give* to another person. Agape is focused on what you can *give* to that person, what need you can meet in that other person. It's not thinking of yourself; it's thinking of others first. Which definition sounds more like God or the example Jesus gave to us? I would choose agape.

Biblical Definition of Love

Agape love is all about giving—giving of ourselves. There are many examples of this from the Bible:

> *John 15:13 – Greater love hath no man than this, that a man lay down his life for his friends.*

> *John 12:25 – He that loveth his life shall lose it; and he that hateth his life in this world shall keep it unto life eternal.*

> *John 13:34 – A new commandment I give unto you, That ye love one another; as I have loved you, that ye also love one another.*

> *1 Peter 4:8 – And above all things have fervent charity among yourselves: for charity shall cover the multitude of sins.*

Arguably, the best definition of love (charity) comes from 1 Corinthians 13. Paul tells us what love is and what love is not:

> *[1]Though I speak with the tongues of men and of angels, and have not charity, I am become as sounding brass, or a tinkling cymbal. [2]And though I have the gift of prophecy, and understand all mysteries, and all knowledge; and though I have all faith, so that I could remove mountains, and have not charity, I am nothing. [3]And though I bestow all my goods to feed the poor, and though I give my body to*

be burned, and have not charity, it profiteth me nothing. ⁴Charity suffereth long, and is kind; charity envieth not; charity vaunteth not itself, is not puffed up, ⁵Doth not behave itself unseemly, seeketh not her own, is not easily provoked, thinketh no evil; ⁶Rejoiceth not in iniquity, but rejoiceth in the truth; ⁷Beareth all things, believeth all things, hopeth all things, endureth all things…¹³And now abideth faith, hope, charity, these three; but the greatest of these is charity.

If you take the list above and make a table that describes what love is and what love is not, you will get something similar to the table below:

Love is...	Love is not...
Patient (suffereth long)	Jealous/resentful (envieth not)
Kind	Boastful (vaunteth not itself)
Assumes the best (thinketh no evil)	Prideful (puffed up)
Truthful (rejoice in truth)	Rude/tasteless/improper (behave itself unseemly)
Reliable (beareth all things)	Self-centered (seeketh not her own)
Encouraging and uplifting, dreams for others, and shows them what they can't see in themselves (hopeth all things)	Angry (not easily provoked)
Protects/preserves (endureth all things)	One to celebrate sin (rejoice not in iniquity)

Paul gives us two lists in this scripture passage. Let's look at them.

"Love Is" items are patient, kind, assumes the best, honest, reliable, encouraging, protecting.

"Love Is NOT" items are jealous, boastful, prideful, rude, selfish, angry, and celebrates sin.

If we look closely at these lists, we can see that the positive "Love Is" descriptors all affect how we treat each other. The negative "Love Is Not" items all center on ourselves. Therefore, God's definition of love is **NOT** focused on "What can I get out of it?" Many people today, like myself, feel attracted to others when they do nice things for us; this makes us feel loved and is then what we call love. It focuses on whether the other person is going to give us what we want. If they do, we say they love us; if they don't, we say they don't love us, and therefore we don't do things for them and don't love them either.

God's love is *other* focused. Our definition of love is *self*-focused. When I say, "I love pizza,"" what I'm saying is that I like how pizza makes me feel. When I say, "I love you," I'm saying I like what you do for me and how you make me feel. God's definition is different. God says that it's not about what you get; it's about what you give. If you love the way First Corinthians 13 says, the way God's Word defines love, you will be focused on what you can sacrifice to nurture and help this relationship to grow with the other person. To sum it up, what Paul is saying in these verses is that agape love, or charity, is an action we do for others.

Agape Love: Love in Action

Now that you know that charity is defined as a willing action to help meet the needs of others while expecting nothing in return, can you do a self-evaluation? Do you love like that? How great a world it would be if we all acted this way everywhere, all the time.

Agape/charity, when we focus on what we can give to meet a need, is a choice; it's not a feeling, unlike eros and philia, where it is an attraction. When we choose to love others because of a feeling, we are building love on a premise that cannot endure. The problem comes when that feeling runs out. Remember when you are first dating? You would think about that person all the time, and you would come up with ways to "win them over" or meet their needs. Perhaps it was the gifts you bought or perhaps it was the element of surprise when picking them up for a mystery night on the town. Whatever it was, that won them over; you *chose* to do those things.

When Cheri and I were dating, we would surprise one another with loving actions all the time. When I graduated with my master's degree, she arranged for a 1957 Chevy limo to pick us up at my house and chauffeur us to dinner, where her entire family was waiting to celebrate my achievement. It was one memorable night! When she went to California to visit her sister, I bought a bag of balloons, filled them with helium, and spread them all over her apartment. When she got home, she was so excited to walk into a room filled with balloons and a giant WELCOME HOME sign! Those actions were examples of us choosing to make each other feel loved.

You need to continue to do those things you did in the beginning of a relationship. You need to take ACTION and show your love by meeting that need and not expecting them to do *anything* in return. Agape love is choosing to serve the needs of others without expectation of anything in return.

Our church has greeters, people who welcome new and returning church members with salutations and help to guide people where they need to be. The greeters are people demonstrating agape love by freely choosing to serve the needs of these new or returning church members. They are meeting the needs people have, and they don't expect anything in return. They don't get paid, and they don't do it expecting people to be friendly. In fact, I've served in this role before, and for the most part, people were appreciative, but I have had more than one person ignore me, scowl at me, and not treat me very well. I didn't complain or let it get me down. Why? Because I wasn't doing it for their accolades; I did it because I wanted to serve in the church. I wanted to show love like God shows us.

This is the type of love that Christ gave as an example to us and his disciples in John 13:12–15:

¹²So after he had washed their feet, and had taken his garments, and was set down again, he said unto them, Know ye what I have done to you? ¹³Ye call me Master and Lord: and ye say well; for so I am. ¹⁴If I then, your Lord and Master, have washed your feet; ye also ought to wash one another's feet.¹⁵For I have given you an example, that ye should do as I have done to you.

In verse 15 above, Christ tells his disciples that he is washing their feet (v. 12) as an example to them. Jesus Christ, our Lord and Master, loves us by meeting our needs. In this case, Jesus washed their feet, but he tells us to "do what I had done to you." He is commanding us to follow his example, to love other people, to meet their needs. There is definitely a connection between love and needs. Loving actions (meeting someone's needs) produce loving feelings (closeness or unity).

It takes a mature Christian to choose to take loving action toward others, to decide to show agape love. Today's society cheapens the word love. They don't understand it. That is why we have children without fathers or mothers and we have broken families and marriages. I lived through it as a child and emulated it as an adult. If you are reading this and saying, "Wow, that's hard to do," I agree. We all struggle with it. But keep reading because chapter 3 will explain how we are able to love like Jesus Christ.

2

THE PHASES OF A RELATIONSHIP

It was a warm summer day, and I was attending my best friend's 17th birthday party. I didn't know anyone beyond my friend's immediate family. My best friend's father was cooking burgers on the grill, and his mother was busy attending to everyone's needs. The adults were sitting around the picnic table talking, and the kids were all in the swimming pool playing Marco Polo, including my best friend's cousin. As the day went on, my best friend was busy opening gifts and talking to aunts and uncles, and I was left alone. His cousin introduced herself to me. I really appreciated how she went out of her way to make me feel comfortable. From that moment on, I started looking at her differently. Her kind heart and consideration for others made me interested in her as a friend. As we talked more, I discovered we had a lot in common, including cracking jokes, being sarcastic, watching movies, and listening to music. Before the party ended, she gave me her phone number, and we talked on the phone almost every day.

I couldn't believe how much we had in common. Our interests were very similar. She was easy to talk to, and every conversation made me discover some new commonality. The more I found we had in common, the closer I felt to her. Occasionally, we would go on a date. I didn't have a car, so our dates consisted of group events at my best friend's house or meeting at the mall. When we were together, we would hold hands and walk around the mall, and I would buy her lunch at the food court. We felt very close to each other. It was a wonderful time in the relationship. The more we had in common, the more we did for one another and the more excited we were for this relationship.

As time went on, the excitement began to fade. There wasn't much more to discover about each other. The relationship wasn't new anymore. The things that once drew us close were happening less and less often. We were still happy with each other and our relationship, but the newness had ended. Where at one time I couldn't wait to call her and talk to her, now I found other things were more important, and the calls became less frequent. Eventually she challenged me, mentioning that we weren't as close as we used to be and that I needed to show her the attention I once did. I tried to explain that I was busy, that other things were keeping me occupied. She got angry because of my excuses, and I got angry because she didn't understand me.

This was our first disagreement. Up until then, she was perfect in every way. But now fear gripped me tight. My parents used to yell and scream at each other when I was young. It upset me as a child, and it made me angry as a young teen. I knew this wasn't what relationships were supposed to be like. My childhood memories of parents fighting and then divorcing convinced me that this disagreement was a glimpse into my future. If I continued this relationship, it would end in misery. We would never get along; we would be destructive to one another. As my anxiety increased, my discomfort with the relationship also increased, and sooner rather than later, we broke up.

Throughout my early adulthood, this pattern was repeated over and over. I would meet someone, we would hit it off, and the relationship would be exciting until the newness waned or until some stressor hit. Then, out of fear, I would end the relationship. As I was searching for that happily ever after, it was a vicious cycle that I couldn't escape. I was searching for that perfect relationship, where no one ever disagreed or fought with each other—a relationship where we continually discovered new, exciting things about each other for all eternity. That was my vision for my happily ever after.

One day the vicious cycle of ending a relationship every time it became difficult came to a sudden stop. I was 21, nearing the end of my Navy enlistment, ready for college, and excited for "my" plans when the girl I was seeing told me she was having a baby. My brain screamed, "I'M NOT READY FOR THAT! This will ruin my plans." All the red lights and sirens were going off in my mind to run, to end the relationship just like all those other times before. But this time, *my* happiness was not the only factor; now I had a child to consider. This innocent child would be impacted to a depth I couldn't fathom if I wasn't able to make the relationship work with his mom.

All those scare-tactic public service announcements from high school came flooding back: "Raising a child can cost as much as $200,000." "You won't be able to go to college if you have a child." The purpose of that public service announcement was truly to scare teenagers from having unprotected sex that resulted in a child. I didn't know it at that time, but having a child wouldn't ruin "my" plans. College was certainly feasible, and yes, raising a child is expensive, but those public service announcements were misleading. Most people have health insurance to mitigate some of the cost, and there may be less costly options to commercial daycare centers. These ads weighed heavily on my mind. Fear had an endless grip on me. My head was telling me to walk away, while my heart said to make it work.

After days and weeks of soul searching and talking to friends, parents, my girlfriend (the mother to be), and those I trusted, I finally made a decision. This time I wanted to work through the stressor in my life. This time I wouldn't run. This time the relationship would succeed, and no matter what, I was going to make it work. If I had to make my own sacrifices I would because, after all, that's what a parent is supposed to do, right? It wasn't fair for a child to be born in a home without a mommy and daddy living together. This innocent unborn baby didn't ask for this, so I would do whatever I could to ensure this relationship lasted forever. In my mind, I had a plan to make us BOTH work through this: We would get married. Marriage was the answer! Marriage would make us both try harder. Marriage would be the fuel for this relationship and help us endure the hard times. Peace and happiness would follow our marriage and bring normalcy to this chaotic relationship. Why not? We were happy once before; marriage would make us happy forever.

I bought a ring, and my girlfriend and I talked. She didn't know what to expect. She was scared. Would I walk away? Was I going to be there for her and the child? Well, she didn't expect a proposal, that's for sure! I asked her, "Will you marry me?" and she responded with "Are you sure?" I fully expected this to be a resounding and joyful "Oh YES!" What I thought was a grand gesture of my commitment turned into a disappointment in her reaction. All I got was a lukewarm response. Even though I was disappointed, I would still see this through. We got married and would make this work.

After getting married, we moved in together. I needed to help prepare for the baby, and we needed to save money. Our baby boy was born. Being a dad was exciting. I had a new appreciation for unconditional love. It wasn't scary like those ads had said it would be. The baby was a drain on resources, but with the help of veteran benefits, we still found money in the budget for me to attend college.

Soon the stress increased. A newborn adds stress to even the strongest relationships. We were new to this parenting thing, and we were exhausted. We attempted to continue dating (baby in tow) but couldn't go anywhere for long without the baby being fussy. Between working full time, going to college, and helping out with the baby, I was stressed, and my energy was depleted. The attention I used to give her became less and less. Typically, when we are under stress, we tend to think more selfishly. That was exactly what I did. Eventually we began drifting apart. I was too tired to attempt to meet her needs, and in response, she stopped meeting my needs. We began drifting apart and felt more like roommates.

To help make ends meet, I was working a night shift, which paid more money, and I took college classes during the day. When I came home, she was asleep; before I woke up, she was gone. On the weekends, we would try to squeeze in something fun to do together, but those days of staying up late with our friends or spontaneous overnight trips couldn't happen with a baby. We went from being too tired to meet each other's needs to completely resenting one another. She didn't feel like I did enough around the house, and she never appreciated the things I did do. Eventually I stopped trying to please her, but I stayed for our son. Every time I thought about throwing in the towel, I would look at my son and think, *I can't do that to him. I can't put him through what I went through.* The stress continued throughout that first year, and eventually the lease was up on our apartment. She told me she didn't want to continue living together, that the relationship just wasn't working. In my heart, I knew it was true, but I couldn't admit defeat. I was miserable. I dreaded seeing her because it was just more stress and anguish.

In my pit of despair, I could see no way out. Reaching to those same worldly sources of wisdom, the same theme began to appear no matter who I spoke to. They all said to show her I love her, tell her I love her, and do more romantic things for her. With every ounce of determination I could muster, I did just that. I bought flowers. I left notes in her lunch. I did more chores around the house. I took her on dates. It seemed to be helping. The fighting was less frequent. The stress decreased a little. Life wasn't as miserable as it was at the pit of the relationship, but it never rose to the levels of happiness we had at the very beginning.

The next phase of our relationship was a series of ups and downs. There were moments of gladness, but ultimately, we were two people who, for the most part, weren't very happy with one another. This went on for months until eventually she met someone else. The hope of renewed happiness and feelings of newness permeated her heart. She told me she didn't think we would ever work out, that I didn't make her happy anymore, and that there was someone else that could do what I could not. The relationship ended. Eventually I conceded that it was the right choice to make. I was alone and depressed and now a single dad. At least my life was more peaceful.

The Phases of Relationships

What I've just described I've heard from many people that were products of divorce and ended up being divorced themselves. There is a cycle to every relationship that starts strong as loving actions lead to mutual attraction (infatuation). Everything is going fine (honeymoon) until some stressor hits the relationship. The excitement fades (dilapidation), and attraction becomes apathy and, in some cases, bitterness (stagnation). No one wants to stay miserable, so the couple decides to rekindle what they once had (recovery).

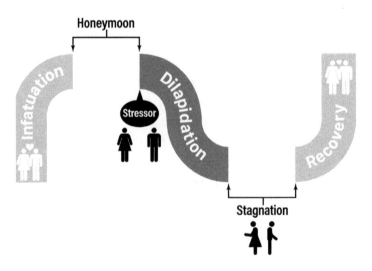

Let's apply these phases to my first marriage, as explained above:

1. *Infatuation* started when we met and were excited about the newness of the relationship and discovering things about one another.

2. The *honeymoon phase* started when there wasn't much more to discover about one another. We still had fun together, but the newness and excitement were wearing off.

3. *Dilapidation* started when she introduced a *stressor* to our relationship: our unplanned pregnancy. We had a lot more stress on our relationship dealing with planning for a child and a wedding at the same time. Feelings of insecurity would occupy my thoughts constantly: *I'm too young to be a dad. Is she the right one for me? I don't want this child to grow up in a broken home like I did.* Things weren't as fun as before, and the fear from my insecurity made us argue over little things that were completely unrelated. Fights happened more and more often, but we both chalked them up to this new stress in our life.

4. *Stagnation* occurred shortly after the baby was born. It was an exciting time, but as I said, a newborn adds stress to any relationship. The stress of a second job and college classes didn't help either. She was saddled with more responsibility for the baby, and I was too tired to put on a smile and try to work it out. We fought every day. This is what I referred to as my "pit of despair."

5. The *recovery phase* started when I willfully decided to make a change to help out more and be more romantic.

Let's look at the five phases of this phenomenon in more detail.

Phase 1: Infatuation

This world will define love as an ooey gooey lovey feeling—emotional butterflies and fireworks as a woman enters a room in her little black dress or a stud with six-pack abs and a witty sense of humor. Many people confuse these butterflies and fireworks with love. This is not love but lust.

This phase of a relationship is called infatuation. Infatuation in the Oxford Dictionary is defined as "an intense but short-lived passion or admiration for someone." During infatuation, the feelings of love are more accidental, reactionary, or chemical in nature. It's been called "puppy love" by some. If you have ever owned a puppy, you know they love to play *all the time*. As puppies, they want attention all the time. Infatuation is the same way. The love is new, and this newness is exciting and different. People experiencing infatuation don't want that feeling to end, just like puppies never want to stop playing.

My high school and college dating life was full of infatuation. Feelings of euphoria would overwhelm me as I explored each new relationship. In the beginning, I felt like the good times would never end, and I just wanted to play all the time. I believed what I saw on television and in the movies: that there was one true love for me and that when I met her, we would live happily ever after. Problems started happening in a relationship because she just wasn't *the one*. In the infatuation phase, people believe the depths of discovering new things is boundless and believe in happily ever after.

People are naturally attracted to other individuals that meet their needs. The devil wants us to believe that this is love. He wants us to fall into his trap. In actuality, that feeling is just "hope or expectation of a need being met."

Take this example, ladies: A man comes along who is charming—opening doors, dressing nice, generously buying flowers and jewelry, and taking you to fancy restaurants. Why do you "fall" in love? Because he is meeting a basic need that all men are supposed to meet: He will provide for me, he will adore me, and he will treat me like a princess forever. Isn't that what most women want? Without realizing it, you start to believe this is the way it will always be, and you create a fantasy that no man can ever attain.

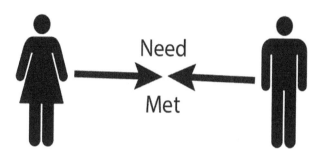

There is a connection between meeting needs and feeling loved. People are naturally attracted to others that meet their needs. This is what is happening in infatuation: The other person is constantly meeting our needs, and therefore the feelings of love continue to attract these two people together.

Remember the beginning of your relationship? You met someone, and you were attracted to one another. Why? Well, you saw something in that person, either something they did or said, that made you feel like they would continue to meet that need in your life. With my wife, it was several things: She was attractive, she was funny, and, most of all, she had a kind heart. She was always thinking of other people and telling me to consider their feelings when I wasn't really thinking too much about their feelings. Consider the following graphic. On the left side are actions taken by my wife that made me feel special, made me feel needed, and made me feel loved. She admired me, she told me I was smart, and she always asked my advice, which made me feel useful. All men have a desire to fix things and take care of people, so she met that need, and I drew closer to her. Every time she complimented me or asked me to do something useful, I was more attracted to her because I felt my needs were being met.

She said I was smart.

He told me I looked good today.

She asked me to fix her car door that squeaked.

He bought me nice flowers.

Marriage

On the other side of the equation, when I complimented Cheri, when I took her on dates, or when I came over with flowers, all those things met her needs and made her feel more attracted to me. Eventually we continued to meet one another's needs, and we became so close that we never wanted it to end; I proposed marriage.

Phase 2: Honeymoon

We were now in the honeymoon phase. After the newness of a dating relationship wears off, infatuation turns into the honeymoon phase. This phase is when the good feelings are still there and we continue to meet each other's needs but the frequency is starting to diminish because everyday life is happening. Our efforts may wane as the other person meets our needs less and less often and selfishness starts to settle in.

The infatuation phase of a relationship is awesome, but no healthy relationship can stay in that phase forever. All things start to deteriorate with time. For example, when I bought my first new car, I would wash it weekly and park it far away from other cars so no one would ding my doors. Eventually, as the newness wore off, I started parking the closest I could to the front door, and the car washing decreased to monthly. The car still made me happy, but I wasn't as excited about it as I was when it was new. At some point, feelings wane, and if you don't take care of the relationship by continuing to show loving actions, it will start to decay. In the honeymoon phase, words are starting to be said out of obligation more than out of feeling. The excitement diminishes as the relationship persists. We are still happy but not as excited.

Phase 3: Dilapidation

Dilapidation begins when the excitement fades. At some point, a stressor will come into the relationship. It could be something major like a new baby or new job or just regular life. Regardless of the reason, reality sets in. If we don't continue to give to each other and put the other's needs first, the relationship will decay.

Remember our example from earlier about the woman in the little black dress who turned your head and the sexy stud with the six-pack abs? Well, at some point, the sexy stud may turn into Captain Sweatpants, his gifts of flowers and jewelry become gift cards, and the fancy dinners turn into take out. Guys, your woman may have had a child and is now 10 years older; that little black dress doesn't fit anymore. Maybe she stopped laughing at your jokes, or she started to ask her father to fix things around the house instead of you.

Reality hits—fantasy over.

So what are we thinking? "Well, I'm just not as attracted to him as I once was," or "She isn't the same woman I married." The problem isn't what we look like or what they buy us! The problem is that one spouse stopped giving and stopped meeting the needs of the other. Maybe he doesn't feel like showing her love because he feels unappreciated and she is critical of everything he does. Maybe she is asking her dad to fix things around the house because he procrastinates so much. This perception of a "fading interest" is really just a lack of motivation to meet your spouse's needs.

The signs of a relationship beginning to dilapidate are clear if you are aware of what to look for. One day you come home from work and you just want to relax. You don't really "feel" like talking to your wife, because you've had a stressful day and you are exhausted. You may not have said a word to her, so she feels ignored and, in return, shows you a little less love.

Take a look at the next diagram. One night I may stop saying the meal was good; after all, I think she knows I like her cooking, and she doesn't need to hear it. Then she is offended and heart-broken, and she stops showing me respect. Perhaps she asks me, "Do you think we can afford that?" questioning my ability to take care of the finances. Then I am offended because I feel that she doesn't trust my ability to lead the family. I yell goodbye across three rooms when I leave the house instead of finding her and kissing her goodbye. All of a sudden, she is asking her father for advice on fixing things around the house, or worse, she is asking him to do it instead of you. You "drift apart" by not meeting needs just like you grew together by meeting those needs.

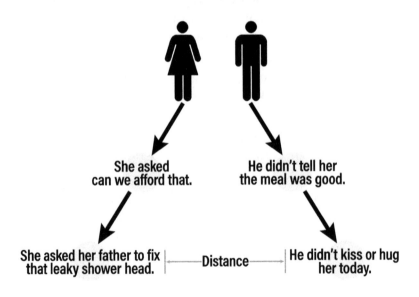

When I first became a father and decided that marriage was the next step, I was determined to work through the stressor in my life. I was going to try to fuel the relationship and endure the hard times. I thought marriage was the answer, but then the relationship began deteriorating. It was deteriorating due to the stress of work, school, and being a new dad. I was constantly thinking more selfishly. My loving actions happened less and less often as stress loomed over the relationship like a dark cloud.

Since I wasn't doing those loving things in the relationship, eventually she stopped doing them for me. Once in a while, we would go out and have fun, but it just wasn't at the same level of happiness it once was. I would try to make her laugh, but my jokes would fall flat or not get the reaction I expected. Where we once were trying to out-give one another, now we were keeping score of how much we were investing in the relationship: Why should I try when she obviously doesn't care anymore? Unmet expectations kept us spiraling down.

According to marriagepoll.com, "The individual factors most commonly leading to divorce include…fading interests in each other." Fading interest is what happened in the dilapidation phase. After months and years of disappointment of that hope not being fulfilled, people realize that what they once thought would never end is over. Prince Charming tells his last funny joke, she gets on his case all the time, and we think our needs will never be met again by our spouse. So we move on, assuming we just aren't compatible.

This is the basic problem with the world's definition of love. Infatuation runs out. We start to think we just don't "love" them anymore. In reality, your interest simply faded because they stopped meeting your needs. We call that falling out of love. Dilapidation is when the process of falling out of love begins and unmet expectations keep the relationship spiraling down until it can't get much worse. The relationship is now moving from dilapidation to an even worse phase: stagnation.

Stage 4: Stagnation

During the infatuation and honeymoon phases, we were meeting each other's needs and moving closer and closer together. During the dilapidation phase, we begin to lose the momentum we once had. We stop meeting the needs in our spouse, yet we continue to expect our spouse to meet our needs as they once did. This causes us to feel unloved because a need that was expected to be met is no longer being met. This will cause a couple to pull apart from one another, and distance creeps in. At the lowest point of dilapidation, we move into what I call stagnation.

Stagnation happens when two people have given up on meeting each other's needs. We start to "learn" that no matter what we do, nothing will change. Our attitudes become "Well, I'm stuck, so I guess I'm doomed to be unhappy." Feelings of hopelessness, loneliness, and depression may set in, and we aren't sure how to get out of this valley we find ourselves in.

Out of desperation, we try to do grand gestures to see a spontaneous return to the honeymoon phase. When that doesn't work, it makes us feel hopeless and less likely to try in the future.

When I was trying to recover from our stagnation in my first marriage, I asked for worldly advice on how to recover. My friends and relatives told me to do some grand gesture of love. Based on that advice, I went out and bought his and her bicycles with a child seat. She would always complain we didn't "go out" enough, and she enjoyed physical exercise. I bought the bikes, assembled them, installed the car seat, and waited with excitement for her to get home so I could surprise her with this grand gesture. I was thinking, *I'm so in tune with her, and she will appreciate all my efforts!* She liked the bikes, and we went out on a ride almost immediately. My son also liked it. I remember him hitting me on the back and giggling as we rode down the trail together. It didn't take long for that feeling to wear off though. Whenever I'd suggest we go for another bike ride together, she would make up an excuse why she couldn't. The same old arguments happened.

As the stress of day-to-day life with a baby hit us again, we were back to disappointment and disagreement. She didn't think I did enough to help, and I felt like she didn't appreciate the effort I gave. I thought my one grand gesture would rebound our relationship to the good old days. That grand gesture was a fading memory. We never rode those bikes again.

One grand gesture will not make things better. It took time to get into the stagnation phase, so it will take consistency and commitment over a long period of time to get out. Lack of expectation management will lead to further frustration and hopelessness. It was unrealistic for me to expect that buying bikes would return us to infatuation. Although it was a great day and I will cherish the memory of my infant son smacking his little arms against my back and giggling behind me as we rode along that trail, that one gesture wasn't enough to sustain those once happy feelings. The need I was trying to fulfill wasn't the need she had. She was overwhelmed and wanted more help from me. When I did help out, she gave me no credit and was critical. We were in a downward spiral that one bike ride couldn't fix. Remember my earlier example of bringing video games to a homeless man? This was the same situation. She wanted more help, and I bought her a bike. But I didn't realize that at the time, and I was upset because my efforts didn't produce the closeness I expected.

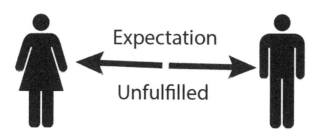

If we only act a certain way to get a certain response, we will most likely be disappointed. Sometimes the one action will take a while to return the response we are expecting. If I cut the grass when I notice it's high and then I come inside, chest puffed up, eagerly awaiting my wife to say, "Oh, honey, you are the best. Thank you so much for taking care of the lawn," and she doesn't say it, I will surely be disappointed. And I can pretty much predict that I won't be so eager to repeat that behavior. Pretty soon I may not do much of anything around the house because I didn't get the response I was hoping for. From that point forward, when my wife asks me, "Why don't you help?" I may think, *But I already tried doing things for you, and you don't appreciate me.* It's like growing a flower. If you watered it one day and the next day you expected to see a bloom, you may feel frustrated and wonder why it didn't work after watering it one time. Now, you and I both know that watering a plant one time will not produce a flower immediately, but you get my analogy. Unfortunately, as married couples, we tend to expect our spouses to immediately respond the way we want them to after one grand gesture. Married couples tend to have unrealistic expectations. Sometimes we need to repeat the actions again and again to get the results we want.

When you meet the needs of others, you are showing Christ-like qualities in your life. The Bible says we love God because he first loved us (1 John 4:19). He first served our needs by giving us His Son; now we show our love to God by taking care of God's people. Love creates more love. When people meet our needs, we move closer to those people, and in return, we want to meet their needs and to make them as happy as they make us.

There is a connection between loving actions and loving feelings. We are naturally attracted to people that meet our needs. To show a love like God shows us, we must be charitable, loving—agape. Another way to say we are meeting the needs of another person is to take on the role of a servant. A servant serves the needs of others, so putting agape love into action is acting like a servant.

In Mark 10:43–45, Jesus tells us that we are to act like a servant or, in other words, to minister unto the needs of others:

> *But so shall it not be among you: but whosoever will be great among you, shall be your minister:* *[44]* *And whosoever of you will be the chiefest, shall be servant of all.* *[45]* *For even the Son of man came not to be ministered unto, but to minister, and to give his life a ransom for many.*

The problem with expectations is that we find ourselves performing actions while assuming we will receive a reward. This is precisely why we become disappointed. We are expecting a reward from someone who is just as imperfect as we are. Every one of us is imperfect. Imperfect people produce imperfect and unpredictable results. If a hope or expectation of someone meeting our needs is not met, then we start to feel hopeless.

> *Proverbs 13:12 – Hope deferred maketh the heart sick: but when the desire cometh, it is a tree of life.*

We get heartbroken, get disheartened, and feel hopeless, all of which are common in stagnation. In my first marriage, I didn't understand the connection between love and meeting needs. Our steam eventually ran out, and we stopped meeting those needs in each other. The problem with infatuation is that it is fueled by the wrong source: our feelings, our hearts. So I fell in love with my first wife because she met my needs. It had nothing to do with agape love and nothing to do with giving and expecting nothing in return. Our whole marriage was based on how we felt. We met each other's needs out of an appreciation for the other person meeting our needs. We reciprocated a giving behavior. But the problem is that those feelings ran out.

We pulled apart as quickly as we came together. We stopped meeting each other's needs. The honeymoon phase was over. We stopped trying as hard because the "feeling" just wasn't there anymore.

Meeting someone's needs is a choice, and true love, agape love, is about meeting that need regardless of how we feel. I realize now that when I said, "I do," to my first wife, I promised to meet those needs no matter how I felt, no matter what the circumstances; that is what "for better or worse" means. I vowed to my first wife and to God that I would continue to choose "love" despite my feelings. If we had both been closer to God and understood the connection between love and needs, the marriage may not have ended.

Perhaps you are thinking, *What are the needs of my spouse? I don't even know how to restore this marriage.* The rest of this book is focused on discovering those needs, telling you what the Bible says about your duties to your spouse, describing their needs, and helping you to talk to your spouse (or prospective spouse) about their needs.

If you don't meet the needs of your spouse, then someone else will. Someone else will soon be providing that "ooey gooey" love feeling. She will be drawn toward him and desire him, not you. Maybe at first it's not physical; it's just a friendship that is known as an "affair of the heart" (Matt. 5:28). You need to be careful. Stop the insanity of dilapidation and stagnation, and humbly go to God and ask him to help you to meet your spouse's needs again.

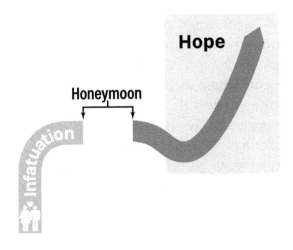

Loving feelings are the result of other people's loving actions. Those loving actions make us feel closer, and the more loving actions we receive, the more hope or expectation there will be of continued future actions. During the infatuation phase, our hope makes us believe that these actions will continue forever.

After my son was born and his mother and I were married, my son's mother met someone who gave her the attention that I didn't. This person was meeting needs that I wasn't. She was happy around this other person, and she thought she was in love. Meanwhile, I was still trying to meet her needs, but our relationship had its ups and downs and was stressful at times. She had a happiness in this new relationship she "hoped" would last. It certainly seemed better than our relationship was at the time. So she ended our relationship (the difficult one) and traded it in for a better relationship (the new one). She eventually married that man, had a child with him, and a few years later divorced him. The pattern continued. Why? Because the worldly definition of love— the hopes and dreams, the butterflies and ooey gooey feeling we get—is worldly love. When that feeling runs out, when that hope runs out, and when the butterflies and ooey gooey feeling end, so does the relationship.

The world's definition of love is based on the "hope" that loving actions will continue forever. The world wants you to believe that the perfect person exists and that once you find them, you will never fight (no stressors). Even if you do encounter trouble, the world will insist that you will overcome it together and that you will persevere no matter what. It's dangerous to base a relationship on the "hope" that he or she just "gets me" and we will never fight. The gray box of hope is an illusion. The reality is that no one can maintain those loving actions forever because they are based on our emotions. The first time our expectations of loving actions don't happen, reality hits us, and we begin to lose hope. As loving feelings fade, the desire to perform loving actions also fades. The world's definition of love is not sustainable, because our emotions are not sustainable.

Phase 5: Recovery

The reality is that stressors do come, and interest will fade in time. The real question is, are you prepared to face them when they do come? After I went through the dilapidation and stagnation of my first marriage, I became depressed. I knew marriage was supposed to be a wonderful thing, but it wasn't for me. Going home from work led to a sense of dread. So rather than go home, I would find reasons to stay at work longer or go out with my friends after work—anything I could do to avoid the reality of a miserable marriage. She didn't seem to mind—probably because she felt the same way. Perhaps she wanted to avoid painful arguments too.

During stagnation, there is existence. I personally know of some marriages that have been in stagnation for 20 years or more. They probably will never get divorced, but they are not very happy, and the quality of their lives and marriages is discontented. Their relationships have all but died, but in the case of my first marriage, it was kept alive out of an obligation to raise a child together. I learned that a shared obligation is not a solid foundation to build a relationship upon.

After weeks and months of being depressed, constant arguing, and feeling like every day was a struggle, I decided that something needed to change. We had to make this better. I didn't know where to turn for answers, but I knew I needed something to help us. We needed our relationship to move toward recovery.

Recovery is about reconnecting. It's about starting to meet those needs again purposefully. Where infatuation is accidental, recovery is about being more purposeful in our loving actions. We make our spouse feel loved by performing actions that meet their specific needs. However, during recovery, we don't become attracted and grow close together as quickly as we do during infatuation. During infatuation, the attraction is more powerful because we have hope that this will continue to last forever. During the dilapidation and stagnation periods, our hope leaves us. We start to despair. Recovery takes longer because there is hurt and offenses, and now there needs to be more time to build trust again.

In my first marriage, we sought psychological marriage counseling. We took advantage of an Employee Assistance Program through my employer to find a counselor. We were offered six introductory sessions, where we were able to meet and talk to the counselor together. My hope was renewed because I believed this man would get to the root of our issues and provide useful tips and strategies that would enable our full recovery. We would actually be happy again. Our son would know what it takes to be in a home where Mommy and Daddy cared for one another, where Mommy and Daddy held hands, snuggled on the couch, and laughed and were best friends.

After only a single session together, the psychologist got to the heart of the problem. My first wife suffered from postpartum depression. She clearly was unhappy, and it wasn't anyone's fault. We needed to blame the circumstances on something, and the psychiatrist told us there was a chemical imbalance that could be treated with medication. So anti-depressant medication was prescribed, and from that point forward, the counselor only wanted to meet with and treat my first wife. I can honestly say I was relieved because prideful Eric just knew that he couldn't have been to blame.

What I didn't realize at the time was that it *was* partially my fault—perhaps even a majority of my fault. The diagnosis from the psychiatrist might have been clinically correct and there may have been an imbalance, but him saying the problem was solely her and blaming it on postpartum depression was not accurate.

So here is where I was at fault: Whenever my authority was challenged as the husband, I would get angry. I would first try to explain the logic behind my decisions, and when that didn't work, I would lash out at her and tell her that I was the husband and I got to make the decisions. In my pride, I would use oppressive behavior to cause arguments and cause her to withdraw and not talk to me, and then was it any wonder she didn't want to be intimate with me? The problem with the psychiatric diagnosis was that I was emboldened by it. I felt the problem was wholly hers and this medicine would be a magic cure, so I just continued to be domineering. What I have learned is that my behavior, my lack of concern for her needs, and my lack of initiative crushed my ex-wife's spirit. These three behaviors took all hope from her.

We both saw small changes at first, and our happiness level increased. Through medication and sheer willpower, we started climbing out of our stagnation. We acted better toward one another. The frequency of our loving actions increased and caused a minor repair in our relationship. However, it never reached the heights of happiness we first felt.

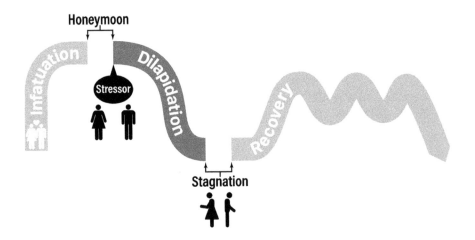

Depicted above is what my first marriage looked like. We recovered from our stagnation but never found true happiness like we had at first. From that point forward, we would have our ups and downs, good days and bad days, but we never truly had a great marriage.

After getting better for a while, we would slip back into stagnation. The psychiatrist's methods didn't work. The medicine didn't work. Laying the blame on her didn't work. We needed more.

The psychiatrist's recommended methods were aimed at treating each other better. We were instructed to do nice things for one another but to do it in our own willpower. Just like being on a strict diet and cutting out sugar completely, it's almost impossible to do in our own willpower. In hindsight, our marriage was never built on the foundation of God, and therefore it couldn't last. The Bible defines a godly marriage, and when you base a marriage on anything but God, you are standing on shaky ground.

We stayed together out of obligation rather than loving actions. Instead of trying to meet the other's needs, we partially met only some needs because the fuel source was our own willpower. We both wanted to raise our son with a "normal" family, with a mom and dad in the same home. We both wanted financial stability created by a two-income family. We thought we were doing the right thing by staying together.

When we try to meet the needs of others in our own power, we will most likely turn a corner toward happiness. We can recover, just not fully. We can choose to meet each other's needs in our own willpower because it's the right thing to do. We are normally able to sustain this effort until we get hurt. We have a tendency to pull within ourselves when we are hurt (flight) or to get contentious (fight). Neither of these reactions helps. They prolong stagnation or further add to the stressor of dilapidation and cause further dilapidation in the marriage.

After only a few more months of counseling, of the ebb and flow of good and mostly bad, our relationship ended in divorce. Foolishly, I believed divorce would make my life easier, happier, and less stressful. It did reduce my stress, but I just replaced one type of pain for another. Prior to divorce, my life contained anger and stress, but now it contained loneliness and despair. Sorrow enveloped my new life along with feelings of failure and hopelessness.

When my son was with me, I was happy, but when he was gone, it was lonely. At night in the darkness, when I was alone, I would ponder, *Where did I go wrong, and what more could I have done? The Bible says divorce is wrong, so will God forgive me? If God doesn't believe in divorce, then why was my marriage so miserable?* All of these depressed thoughts were swirling through my mind.

After returning to church, I started feeling hopeful again. I read my Bible and prayed to Jesus. I learned and applied biblical truth to my life, and I started to restore the relationship I once had with Jesus Christ. After a few months, God revealed something about me and my marriage.

My first marriage failed because God was not present. We did not have a relationship with Jesus, and therefore we didn't have a strong marriage. What I thought at the time was our recovery wasn't really. The marriage was surviving, but it wasn't thriving. The main reason was because we were running the marriage on the wrong fuel source. As I said earlier, the recovery phase is more intentional than the infatuation phase, but the power of the flesh (willpower) is nothing compared to the power of the Spirit (God's power). Where willpower can help a marriage survive, the power of God through the Holy Spirit can take you to heights you never thought imaginable that only God can supply: a happy, thriving, unified marriage.

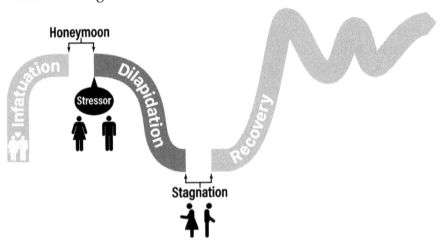

In this graphic of the five phases, you can see that God can help your marriage become even better than it was the day you said, "I do."

During the recovery phase, you have three choices to end a stagnant relationship:

1. Do things in your own will (keep it as is)
2. End the relationship (divorce)
3. Turn it over to God (make a change)

After trying the first two, I realized that the third option was the only way to go. I realized that we all have spiritual needs. Those needs are fulfilled through our one need, Jesus Christ (Phil. 4:19). The next chapter will dissect this more fully, but just remember, we need to put our entire trust in God.

The story of Job and the story of Habakkuk both had a crisis of faith. They both backslid or doubted God when their circumstances were bad. However, when they trusted God and put their faith in him despite their circumstances, they had a spiritual explosion far greater than anything they had accomplished earlier:

Job 13:15 – Though he slay me, yet will I trust in him: but I will maintain mine own ways before him.

You can throw your hands up in the air in frustration, saying, "Why me, God?" or you can throw your hands up in adoration and ask, "What would you have me learn, God?" My first time through marriage, I was frustrated with God, and my pride got in the way of understanding him, just like Job and Habakkuk, but when I came humbly before him, I started to learn things that helped bring me peace and stability despite my circumstances.

Habakkuk was frustrated thinking that God had abandoned him:

Habakkuk 1:2 – O LORD, how long shall I cry, and thou wilt not hear! Even cry out unto thee of violence, and thou wilt not save!

When I was in dilapidation, it felt like God wasn't listening. When I was in stagnation, I was hurting, and it seemed like God didn't notice. After my divorce, I was at a low point of my life, wondering if God would even listen to me. The great thing about God is that he loves us no matter how broken we are. He is there for us no matter how bad we screw up, and he is waiting for us with open arms when we are ready to listen.

Habakkuk goes on to complain about his circumstances (Habakkuk 1:6–10). When Habakkuk finally stops and listens, God responds:

> *Habakkuk 2:1 – I will stand upon my watch, and set me upon the tower, and <u>will watch to see what he will say unto me</u>, and what I shall answer when I am reproved.*

> *Habakkuk 2:2 – And the* Lord *answered me…*

Like Habakkuk, when I ran back to church and started listening and applying the Word of God, he answered me. He heard my prayers and helped me the moment I stopped trying to figure out my life on my own and the moment I went to him with humility.

> *Habakkuk 3:2 – O* Lord, *I have heard thy speech, and was afraid: O* Lord, *revive thy work in the midst of the years, in the midst of the years make known; in wrath remember mercy.*

The Lord revived me just like he revived Habakkuk. The power of God's Word will transform your life. If you listen, if you apply it, and if you use it to fuel your marriage, you will reach heights you can only imagine.

3

SPIRITUAL NEEDS

Spiritual needs are the byproducts of having a relationship with Jesus, which comes from God and through godly living. The three needs I place into this category are hope, peace, and joy. Hope, peace, and joy are results of our believing in God through the Holy Spirit.

> *Romans 15:13 – Now the God of hope fill you with all joy and peace in believing, that ye may abound in hope, through the power of the Holy Ghost.*

We are all born with a sin nature. This sinful nature makes us selfish and inclines us to put our own needs first. The Bible describes our sinful nature as "fleshly desires." These fleshly desires come to us naturally, and it's difficult to put other's needs before our own—but it's not impossible.

We all know being selfish is wrong, and when we put our minds to it, we can overcome selfish desires for the good of others. However, this is not sustainable forever. Our willpower is limited. In my first marriage, I tried to recover my marriage by using determination and emotional energy, which was not sustainable.

We can continually fulfill the needs of others through the power of God and his Holy Spirit. When we have the Holy Spirit in us, he convicts us and helps us to be humbler. When we are humbler, we are eager to meet the needs of others.

> *Philippians 2:5–8 – ⁵Let this mind be in you, which was also in Christ Jesus: ⁶Who, being in the form of God, thought it not robbery to be equal with God: ⁷But made himself of no reputation, and <u>took upon him the form of a servant</u>, and was made in the likeness of men: ⁸And being found in fashion as a man, he humbled himself, and became obedient unto death, even the death of the cross.*

Jesus was always putting other's needs over his own. He lived in selflessness, and he lived in the form of a servant.

> *Matthew 20:27 – And whosoever will be chief among you, let him be your servant:*

When we are humble, we bring unity to our marriages. Jesus lived for and thought about other's needs before his own. For God to send Jesus to Earth in human form was the ultimate form of humility. Not only did Jesus humble himself to be born human but once he became human, He embraced humility during his life, the life he created.

God could have chosen any time in human history to send his son Jesus to Earth, but he chose for him to endure the torture of the Romans. The Romans were masterful at torture; they invented scourging and used crucifixion. Roman scourging whips are said to be one of the most painful instruments of torture known to man. Crucifixion is believed to be the worst kind of death that has ever been invented. Jesus humbled himself and took on the punishment of the world's sin so that each of us could live eternally in heaven if we believe in Jesus, admit we are sinners, and know that God sent Jesus to take on our sins that we would escape eternal hell. That is love; that is humility. He never came to be served but to serve us—to save us. His selfless acts were examples to us.

John 13:13–16 – ¹³Ye call me Master and Lord: and ye say well; for so I am. ¹⁴If I then, your Lord and Master, have washed your feet; ye also ought to wash one another's feet.¹⁵For I have given you an example, that ye should do as I have done to you. ¹⁶Verily, verily, I say unto you, The servant is not greater than his lord; neither he that is sent greater than he that sent him.

Jesus took our punishment. He satisfied the wrath of God against our sin and was our atonement. Atonement is defined as "reparation made by giving an equivalent for an injury."[2] Jesus was a sacrifice that God deemed equivalent to all the sins of the world.

The Bible commands us to have the same mindset of Christ:

Philippians 2:5 – Let this mind be in you, which was also in Christ Jesus:

"Let this mind be *in* you" means to make this the model of everything we do. This verse doesn't tell us to go get this mindset. He tells us to adopt it, to put it on. We already have the mindset of Christ, but we need to let it dominate our minds and our thoughts. Jesus Christ brought with him a very distinct mindset. That mindset is powered with the Holy Spirit, who lives within all of us who are believers and should rule us.

The Need for Hope

We all need hope. Hope helps us to perform better in life, attain our goals, and overcome failures.[3] Hopeful people are more likely to form close relationships and keep them. Hope allows us to formulate goals in our lives and achieve them. Without hope, it is difficult to overcome the burdens we face in this continually changing world.

The Bible tells us we are hopeless without Jesus Christ:

---

2 http://webstersdictionary1828.com/Dictionary/atonement

3 Snyder C, Cheavens J, Sympson S. Hope: An individual motive for social commerce. *Group Dynamics: Theory, Research, and Practice* [serial online]. June 1997;1(2):107-118.

Ephesians 2:11–12 – ¹¹Wherefore remember, that ye being in time past Gentiles in the flesh…¹²That at that time ye were without Christ…strangers from the covenants of promise, having no hope, and without God in the world:

Hope is built on faith and gives us courage to understand that despite our circumstances, God will absolutely be there for us and produce good results. The better we know God, the more we have a relationship with God through our Lord Jesus Christ, the more faith we gain, and the more hope we have.

Romans 15:4 – For whatsoever things were written aforetime were written for our learning, that we through patience and comfort of the scriptures might have hope.

Romans 15:4 tells us that hope is the end result of understanding and having faith in the promises of God. When you're going through the storms of life and feel lost, you have the need of hope met by God through Jesus Christ. The more we read our Bibles and pray, the more comfort we will feel because we know the outcome is in the hands of God, and He will produce better results than we can possibly imagine.

A few years after my divorce, I met Cheri, and we married. This time I was strong in my faith. I was a saved Christian with a growing relationship with Jesus. I was praying and reading my Bible regularly. I was going to church faithfully, and so was Cheri. Cheri and I have been married more than 13 years, and the happiness we feel is greater than in my previous marriage, but it's also greater than when we first met. Cheri had a young son, exactly two years and four months older than my youngest son and exactly two years and four months younger than my oldest son. It was as if God was putting two broken families back together again. Praise the Lord that he is in the restoration business. He knows how to make broken people whole again. God knows how to put Jesus in our lives to make us joyful again, and He knows how to take two broken families and make them whole again.

Like other divorced couples that have entered into a blended family, we had our struggles. Those times were stressful but not as bad as the biggest stressors we were about to face. Just over a year into our marriage, while we were still in our honeymoon phase, a stressor was introduced into our household. My stepson, at age 10, started to show the first signs of what we soon learned was Tourette's syndrome.

Cheri and I noticed it during a fall soccer game when he started showing physical tics. He was stretching his neck during the middle of the game while on the field. We asked him about it later. He didn't really have an answer other than "I just feel like I need to do it." After some online research, we ruled out muscle aches and other minor causes, and we were at a loss.

After months and numerous doctor visits, it was confirmed: He had Tourette's syndrome. According to WebMD, "Tourette's syndrome is a problem with the nervous system that causes people to make sudden movements or sounds, called tics, that they can't control. For example, someone with Tourette's might blink or clear their throat over and over again…. Tourette's has been linked to different parts of the brain, including an area called the basal ganglia, which helps control body movements. Differences there may affect nerve cells and the chemicals that carry messages between them."

A.J. would stretch his neck, twirl his tongue, or clear his throat without thinking about it. Sometimes he would even make high-pitched sounds. He could repress it if he tried really hard, but it was very difficult for him to do so. It would be like you or me trying to hold back a sneeze or not scratch an itch. Tourette's is when your brain doesn't have a stop sign to tell you NOT to do that thing or make that noise. We didn't know any of this at first. We didn't understand what this syndrome was, nor did we have any coping strategies.

We spent four years trying to understand this syndrome, searching for others that had developed coping strategies, and then educating others about it. As you can imagine, this was a huge stressor on our marriage, and we went through the seven stages of grief. We first denied it and thought it must be something more minor. Then it was guilt as my wife thought perhaps she had caused it by genetically passing something along. I was under attack from her ex-husband, who blamed me for his son having Tourette's. Next we bargained with God: "Why him and not me?" Then we started to despair. Angry about the injustice to an innocent child, we would lash out at each other while we were dealing with the impact on all of our lives. We didn't understand nor were we educated enough to handle things properly.

In addition to expending energy dealing with day-to-day life, we were also going to support meetings, attending conferences, fighting with/educating the schools, going to doctors' appointments, and even modifying A.J.'s diet. Cheri and I had very little energy left for one another. We didn't date like we used to, and we didn't spend time meeting each other's needs, because we were so focused on this issue. Our youngest son felt neglected because all of our attention was on A.J. The stress of the situation sometimes caused us to snap at each other out of frustration. Cheri didn't want to do anything but talk about the situation.

Since Cheri was working part time, she tended to spend more time on understanding Tourette's than I did. When I got home after working an eight- to ten-hour day, Cheri wanted to talk about what she had learned and how A.J. was doing, not about how my day was. Cheri was too tired and worried about A.J. to focus on our marriage or meet my needs. This made me feel distanced from her, which made me angry. I wasn't angry at A.J.; after all, he certainly didn't choose this. I was angry at the situation and angry at God. I couldn't understand why God would afflict this disorder on a boy who didn't deserve it. Not only was A.J. suffering but so was my wife, Cheri. And now so was I. *Why God? Why?*

That anger toward God pulled me away from him. It put a wall up between Cheri and me too. Cheri admitted that she pulled away from God for the same reason. But in addition to anger, she felt guilt that she had caused this. She calls it "mother's guilt."

She questioned everything about her genetics, the conception, her pregnancy, her delivery, and also the food or medicine she gave A.J. when he was a toddler. Mother's guilt was all in her head, and it was the lies of the devil, who was telling her those things. Satan was doing that in the hopes that it would pull Cheri away from God—and it did exactly that!

We were young in our spiritual walk, and we didn't fully understand God's promises or rely on God's power to help us. When we first got saved, all we wanted to do was serve the Lord, but we did it in our own power, not relying on his power, the power of the Holy Spirit.

Eventually we gained an understanding of Tourette's syndrome and actually developed a few strategies to cope better. However, over that four-year period of not meeting each other's needs, our marriage slowly descended into stagnation. Stagnation in our marriage was caused by a self-reliant and arrogant attitude. Things were dilapidating because we pulled away from God. During storms in our lives, we need more encouragement and more strength that is derived from God and his people. But rather than more church, more Bible reading, and more spiritual fellowship, we instead pulled away from the one who provides comfort. We didn't read our Bible or pray as often because we were so busy and focused on outside circumstances. We lost sight of the most important thing to a strong marriage.

We didn't totally abandon God. We still went to church every Sunday, but you can't have victory in the Christian life by focusing on God and his Word only once a week. We didn't have a servant's heart or the humble mind of Christ. We were operating under our own willpower and thus fulfilling the works of the flesh.

Then a wake-up call occurred. We had always decided that when our children became teenagers, we would allow them to choose whether or not they wanted to go to church. As young adults, I wanted them to make the choice to follow God on their own, not because Mom and Dad told them to go but because *they* chose to develop that relationship with Jesus on their own.

One day I asked my young adult children to come to church with me. When they told me, "No, I'm going to skip church today," that hit me. It hit me harder than any punch in the gut could. It hit me straight in the heart. I asked them why. Why didn't they want to come to church? Why wouldn't they want a relationship with God? It was because my kids (and my wife) didn't see me as a role model anymore. They saw me as someone who went to church once a week and read his Bible once a week yet didn't act any different than the world—no different than their other parents, who didn't go to church at all. They were thinking, *What is church and God really doing for you besides eating up your Sunday?*

I took a long look in the mirror, and I found that even though I was a saved Christian, I wasn't producing the fruits of the Spirit; I was producing works of the flesh. I didn't have joy; I had frustration. I didn't have peace; I had worry. I didn't have longsuffering; I had anger. I chose to handle this lengthy trial in our lives using my own power rather than the power of the Holy Spirit. I was spiritually empty and physically drained.

Cheri admitted to me that she was so angry at God and the circumstances that her bitterness was imprisoning her. She was bitter toward other families that had children A.J.'s age who were "normal." Not only did they have "normal" kids but they didn't have the blended family stress that we had to deal with. Where she was once so happy with the life we were living, now she was mad at God for this life. This was yet another struggle. She would ask God, "Why God? Why did I have to have just one more trial to get through? Haven't I been through enough? Hasn't A.J. been through enough?" She had no hope. No joy. No peace.

There are many Christians today that have the Holy Spirit but choose to ignore the Spirit and succumb to worldly influences (the flesh). Cheri and I did this when we were dealing with A.J.'s Tourette's syndrome. The devil uses worldly influences to destroy relationships with God, just like he attempted to do to Jesus after he fasted 40 days and nights (Matt. 4:1–11).

Galatians 5:19–21 describes the works of the flesh:

19Now the works of the flesh are manifest, which are these; Adultery, fornication, uncleanness, lasciviousness, 20Idolatry, witchcraft, hatred, violence, emulations, wrath, strife, seditions, heresies,21 Envying, murders, drunkenness, reveling, and such like:…and they which do such things shall not inherit the kingdom of God.

Galatians goes on to tell us the fruits of the Spirit in the following two verses:

22But the fruit of the Spirit is love, joy, peace, longsuffering, gentleness, goodness, faith, 23Meekness, temperance: against such there is no law.

We never get rid of our sin nature. It's always there, and once in a while, it will show itself. When you become a Christian, you need to mature. You need to begin developing a mature Christian relationship. While we produce the works of the flesh naturally, we can only produce the fruits of the Spirit through the supernatural power of God, through the Holy Spirit.

If you're thinking this sounds awfully familiar to my first marriage, you are mistaken. There was a big difference between these two stagnation phases. The first time through, this stagnation was without Christ and therefore without hope. I didn't see a way out of the situation, and I didn't see any way to recover from the issues in our marriage. The marriage was hopeless. This time around, I knew the answer. I knew the promises of God, and therefore I knew that he would never leave us nor forsake us (Heb. 13:5). It still scared me, but before, I didn't see a way out; now I had hope by relying on the promises of God. I knew that a humble mind, a servant's heart, and a rededicated focus on him would lead us out of our stagnation. The hope of a better tomorrow and the power of the Holy Spirit gave both of us comfort and helped restore our marriage.

Cheri and I rededicated ourselves and renewed our relationship with Jesus. It was as if we were reborn for a second time after salvation. Through daily prayer and interaction with Jesus, he would help us do good things for one another. As we grew closer to Christ individually, Cheri and I became humbler and had more of a servant's heart toward one another, which made our marriage better. The stronger our relationship with Christ became, the humbler we were, and the more servant-like we became, the stronger our marriage grew. The power source of God started to change us, to transform and renew our minds to focus less on our own needs and more on the needs of each other and our children. We realized we needed Jesus Christ; we needed God. The need for Jesus is essential to being a servant, having humility, and therefore the unity of a strong marriage (Phil. 4:19). The closer we got to Jesus, the closer we got to one another, and our marriage was propelled to new heights like we had never felt before.

Throughout the recovery phase, Cheri and I started doing daily Bible study and meditating on God's Word together. We prayed longer and more effectively. We topically studied through the fruits of the Spirit and contrasted those to the works of the flesh. We memorized verses, spent more time in church, and dedicated our time to godly friends. The result was a thriving marriage with God in the center of it all.

Our studies encouraged us to do more in the Spirit. We began subjecting every thought to the Spirit, and that started producing spiritual feelings. When we submit our thinking and feelings to the Spirit, our actions or inactions are in accordance with God's will. This is how God, from the very beginning, planned for our spiritual lives to work.

Cheri and I rejected the so-called "pleasures of the world." The pleasures of God made us so much happier. In 1 John 2:15–16, we see the means by which the devil tempts us to act in our own will and not God's will. The devil uses the outside influences described in 1 John 2:15–16 to get us to act in our fleshly desires (self-interests), which ultimately destroy our walk with God and, in the long run, make for miserable and selfish relationships:

1 John 2:15–16 – [15]Love not the world, neither the things that are in the world. If any man love the world, the love of the Father is not in him. [16]For all that is in the world, the lust of the flesh, and the lust of the eyes, and the pride of life, is not of the Father, but is of the world.

The Need for Peace

With God, we have hope. No matter what our circumstances, we know that God will produce good results. But we can also have peace despite our circumstances. One way we gain peace is by continually filling our Holy Spirit, allowing us to overcome worldly temptations.

The devil uses the lust of the flesh, the lust of the eyes, and the pride of life to tempt us to follow the desires of our flesh.

The flesh and the Spirit are at war with one another:

Galatians 5:17 – For the flesh lusteth against the Spirit, and the Spirit against the flesh: and these are contrary the one to the other: so that ye cannot do the things that ye would.

This verse in Galatians says that the spirit and the flesh are contrary to, or opposite of, one another. For the saved Christian, there is a war going on inside of us each and every day. When we give in to those temptations to do what we want to do, to get what we want, and to say what we want, we are rebelling against God's will and against God's Spirit, and that is a sin.

When we allow those temptations to influence our minds and emotions, what we're really doing is allowing the devil to diminish our ability to be used of God. The devil doesn't care if we worship him; he just wants to keep us from worshipping God.

Lust of the Flesh

The lust of the flesh is when the natural man (works of the flesh) is being influenced to take action. Have you ever been traveling down the road and someone flies past you? Our natural reaction is to put our foot down on the gas. We may think, *If that guy is doing it, I want to do it too. He might be breaking the law, but he can't get ahead of me.* That is a desire to *do*, a lust of the flesh.

Another example is when we are dieting. You make a New Year's resolution to lose some weight and to eat healthier. But then you are at a party, and seeing other people eating off a plate of cookies, you start to desire to eat those cookies too. The only thing stopping you from eating that cookie is your will. You can choose to act (take a cookie and eat it) or choose not to act (by walking away) by using our own willpower. Sheer willpower is the only thing stopping you from reaching out and eating one of those cookies.

Bad influences in your life can convince you it's okay to give into your temptations. They will tell you, "Go ahead and have a cookie; it's only one. It's okay. Everyone else is eating one. It's a party. Live a little." Perhaps it's not a cookie but a beer. For some people, having a beer can trigger an over indulgence, and one beer turns into two, which turns into a night of drinking and other bad choices and bad consequences. People that encourage you to give into the lust of the flesh (your temptations) and to do the things that may hurt you are not the kinds of friends you should have in your life.

Worldly Temptations

Lust of the Flesh
- Other people doing it.
- Peer pressure.
- Being told "no".
- Inappropriate influences.

Lust of the Eyes
- Advertising.
- Not getting what we want.
- Keeping up with the Joneses.

Pride of Life
- Pop culture.
- Success of others.
- Mistreatment.

One last example that most people don't consider as a temptation is inappropriate media. Media can be books, movies, TV, Internet, newspapers, etc. The Internet is a great tool, but there are a lot of bad things we can let into our homes through the computer. I know there are many people that struggle with pornography. You may think you can look at this one image and it won't affect you, but it does. (You need to keep that stuff away from you because marriages have ended over what started as "one image" that led to an addiction to pornography.) Even TV shows we watch today can be pornographic sometimes. We need to limit what we allow our eyes to see and our ears to hear. Even music lyrics that tell you it's okay to hate, to be angry, or to give into sexual temptations can be dangerous. Books filled with romance that build unrealistic expectations of the behavior of men and women can be damaging to a marriage. The devil uses these forms of influence to convince us that this is how the world really is, to get us to do what we want to do—to give into the lusts of the flesh. The problem is that what we are tempted to do is not what God wants us to do.

Lust of the Eyes

The next category is the lust of the eyes. This is when we see something and want to possess it. The Bible calls this covetousness. We live in a culture full of advertising. Scholars such as Ed Bernays have studied human psychology and are experts at manipulating our emotions through advertising. Ed Bernays was the nephew of Sigmund Freud and was responsible for several successful public relations campaigns that influenced more women to smoke cigarettes, kids to take baths, use of disposable cups, and even eating bacon and eggs for breakfast. Based on his work in the 1920s and 1930s, we now have people tuning into the Super Bowl just to watch the commercials. Commercials today are masterful at making us desire to have what we see. I remember growing up that my parents would fix and patch and do everything they could to keep our lawnmower going. We had that thing for almost 20 years! Today we scratch the paint on our car and we are ready to trade it in for a newer model. Sometimes there isn't a thing wrong with it, but there is some new feature we just have to have.

Some men and women think their spouse should be or look like the people they see in magazines, on TV, or in the movies. I've heard my wife sometimes complain about her own body shortly after seeing an attractive woman on TV. I remind her that is not God's standard of beauty and that I think she is the most beautiful woman in the world. But we are all influenced by the world to feel like we should strive to follow Hollywood's standard.

We need to get ourselves away from the lust of the eyes: the urge to have and to "keep up with the Joneses." We see someone walk by with the newest iPhone, and we think, *I see a small scratch on my screen. I guess I need a new phone.*

The lust of the eyes could be your desire to get the promotion your coworker earned. We've all been there. We were passed over for a promotion, or someone else got the job we wanted. Then we get upset and bitter toward the person that got what we wanted.

There was an experiment performed in 2003 by Emory University's Dr. Frans de Waal, where he had two monkeys in adjacent cages doing tricks and he rewarded them with cucumbers. Part way through the experiment, one monkey was rewarded with grapes rather than cucumbers. Since the grapes were a more desirable fruit, this caused the monkey getting only cucumbers to get angry. At first the monkey dropped the cucumber. Then he grabbed the bars and rattled his cage. Finally, the monkey threw the cucumber back at the person that gave it to him.

When we "see" an injustice in our lives, the lust of the eyes makes us angry and unhappy. It generates strife in our lives. I used to be just like that monkey. I got angry when my staff did not do what I expected of them. I wanted to have family who accepted me for who I was. I wanted my wife to work, take care of the house and kids, and still have energy and time for me. I wanted to have children who followed God even when I wasn't doing it myself. When I didn't get what I wanted (promotions, new cars, a better body, obedient children), I became like that monkey: angry, resentful, and bitter toward others.

Pride of Life

Lastly, we have the pride of life—that feeling of importance. There is a great amount of pressure to be something noteworthy. Just look at pop culture. Athletes and movie stars are worshipped like gods. Back in the '40s, Lou Costello from the comedy team of Abbott and Costello had a net worth of $1 million; compare that to President Roosevelt, whose net worth was $60 million. Compare that to 2017, when President Obama had a net worth of $12 million while Brad Pitt and Payton Manning were worth more than $200 million each. Our athletes and movie stars make more than the people who run our government—the leader of the free world! There is something wrong with that. Most people idolize athletes and movie stars more than our government leaders, our police officers, our firefighters, or our military.

The pride of life is thinking we can do a better job than someone else. Have you ever envied somebody that seems to have it better than you? Perhaps, like me, you have a blended family, and you are looking at the one-marriage family and wishing you had their life. Do you wish you had it together like they do? Do you think, *Why did God give me this situation?* The desire to be something we aren't—a movie star, an all-star athlete, or just someone that seems to have it more together than we do—is the pride of life.

The devil uses these temptations to influence our minds and our emotions. When we start to rationalize why a bad behavior is acceptable, a war is about to begin. The Holy Spirit convicts us, and we think, *No, don't do that,* but then we are tempted by the flesh: "Hey, it's okay. If it makes you feel good, then do it." This is how I ended up having two kids out of wedlock. I was a Christian in name only. A few times a year you would see me at church singing the songs and saying amen, but the rest of the time I was focused on me and my problems rather than God. I was tempted by the sin of premarital sex because I just wanted to feel good, to feel something.

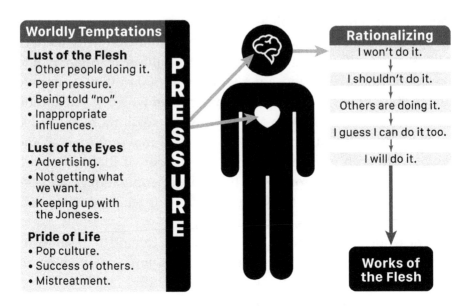

I knew what I was doing was against God, so I tried to date without having intimate relations, but eventually I would give into my desires because the temptation was too strong. Watching people on TV being affectionate would start me rationalizing. The flesh thinks, *It's okay to just kiss someone as long as I don't do anything more. After all, I am a sinner, and I know that other people are doing it. Just one little kiss won't matter.* The problem is that one kiss leads to the desire for more intimate behavior. The Holy Spirit was saying no, but as I continued to rationalize, think, and meditate on that bad thing, I started to desire it in my heart. The minute I removed my mind and emotions from the influence of the Holy Spirit, I gave in. I did my will, not God's will. The voice of the Spirit became barely audible, until all I could hear was my own mind rationalizing my bad behavior, moving from "I won't do it" to "I shouldn't do it" to "Others are doing it" to "I guess I can do it" and eventually to "I will do it." The devil uses this rationalization to make us think what was forbidden is now okay. It is only after we have given into that temptation that we realize the penalty of our sinful action. Just to be clear I am not saying you should abstain from kissing unless, like me, it will lead to a desire for more. We all have our unique struggles and physical intimacy was one of my mine.

Our sinful actions have consequences. Proverbs 5:22 describes how committed sin can put us in chains like Samson:

His own iniquities shall take the wicked himself, and he shall be holden with the cords of his sins.

We may not end up in physical chains but metaphorical chains. When we give into those temptations and commit sin in our lives we end up "holden with the cords" of our sins. Those cords will strangle us spiritually and completely destroy our relationship with God, which leads to destroying relationships with those we love, thus eliminating peace and joy in our lives.

Isaiah 26:3 – Thou wilt keep him in perfect peace, whose mind is stayed on thee: because he trusteth in thee.

God communicates to our souls through the Holy Spirit. Our souls should be subject to the Holy Spirit so that we are doing God's will in our lives. The soul is in a battle between the worldly temptations of the flesh and the Spirit.

If your mind is stayed (focused) on God, then you are tapping into the Holy Spirit and allowing that Spirit to repel the worldly influences. In so doing, you are free to act in God's will and not your own will. That is why we pray, "Thy will be done" (Matt. 6:10). We are praying to God to fill our Spirit and for him to "lead us not into temptation" (Matt. 6:13). When we use God's power to resist temptations, we have peace in our lives. The Holy Spirit is our source of peace:

2 Thessalonians 3:16 – Now the Lord of peace himself give you peace always by all means. The Lord be with you all.

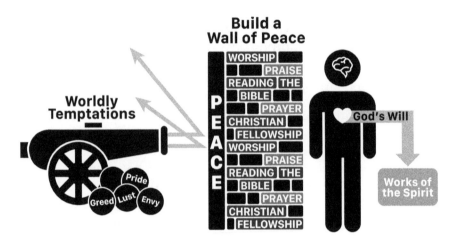

As long as our minds and hearts stay focused on Christ (the LORD of peace), he will be with us and give us peace. Picture the Holy Spirit like a brick wall. The better our relationship with God, the more we will worship, the more we will praise, the more Bible reading we will do, the more we will talk to God through the Spirit in prayer, and the higher our wall will be. We are building a wall of peace by filling our Holy Spirit, therefore repelling those temptations of the devil. Those worldly temptations will no longer appeal to us or be able to influence us any longer. However, if we let the Spirit's influence in our lives dwindle, we will be susceptible to those temptations, so we need to stay focused on God.

That filled Spirit is the source of our peace. Changing our behavior starts by tapping into the power of the Holy Spirit. When I'm filled with the Spirit, those temptations of the flesh don't hold as much appeal to me, and I can resist the temptations of the world as long as my Spirit is full. When we are Spirit-filled Christians we have a buffer against worldly influences.

Every time the devil attacks, that world oppresses us. When we have a stressful situation, a little bit of our Spirit drains from us. The circumstances of this world are constantly draining our Spirit. When we are walking down the hall and someone runs into us with a hot cup of coffee, when someone cuts us off in traffic, or when our kids don't listen, we could easily lose a bit of our Spirit, a bit of our peace. As the day or the week goes on, that wall of peace appears to be crumbling. If we don't spend time every day recharging our Spirit in hymns, prayers, worship, and Bible reading, we won't handle those stressors well.

For some of us that don't have a strong relationship with Jesus Christ, this can be a problem. Some of us have a small wall of peace. Others have holes in their wall. Those of us that have that small or damaged wall will lose our Spirit more quickly than others. I've seen people who sing in worship and praise on a Sunday morning, and as soon as they are at work on Monday, they are acting like the world. For others, it could be when that alarm goes off before work and they are cranky before they even get to the office. For some of us, it's as soon as we are driving home after the church service on Sunday, when we are faced with selfish drivers or strife in the family. I've seen some who will lose their Spirit in the parking lot of the church immediately after the service, cutting people off to get out before them. These are indicators of a weak spiritual influence. We need to continually fill our Spirit through our relationship with God every hour of every day.

The Christian life is all about having a relationship with God. Going to church every Sunday, reading spiritual books, and memorizing and regurgitating Bible verses are not what Christianity is all about. Being a Christian is all about improving our personal relationship with God. That relationship is what is going to change you.

The devil wants us to believe that just knowing right and wrong is enough. Then we try to perform right and wrong in our own willpower, and we fail and get frustrated.

I didn't start going to church until I was in middle school. This was when I began to learn about Jesus and God. The church told me to pray to God, but they never taught me to have a relationship with him. For the most part, I figured out life on my own (or at least I thought I did). My parents didn't encourage me to study God's Word or pray; they encouraged me to do good in school. They stressed that the most important thing in the world was a good education and a good job, so my focus in life was on obtaining good grades or intellectual pursuits.

As we saw earlier, our power source, the Holy Spirit, comes from communicating with God. But for me, my pride got in the way. My belief was that I had all the information I needed to do things my way and that a relationship with God wasn't necessary.

Each day I would pass by my prayer closet and refuse to pray because I didn't have time or didn't think I needed to pray. I was basically telling God, "I got this." I really thought I could have joy and peace in my life through my own power. I assumed that I had knowledge to determine right and wrong, and I would use my own will, not God's will, to make my own decisions. Because of our knowledge, we think we can play God:

1 Corinthians 8:1 – …Knowledge puffeth up, but charity edifieth.

The devil didn't lie to Eve when he told her she would be like God by eating the fruit of the tree of the knowledge of good and evil (Gen. 3:4–5). When we think our version of good and evil is on par with God's, we are acting with pride, we are stealing our own joy, and we are breaking God's heart. The knowledge of good and evil makes us think we know better than the Bible does or, in some cases, makes us think we don't need to read or study it at all. When we think we know how to live our lives better than God does, we are replacing a relationship with the Lord with knowledge.

Our eldest son, Matt attended college in Florida. A few weeks after Christmas, he texted me telling me he had a lot of pain in his mouth. His wisdom teeth were coming in, and he wanted the dental insurance information. I immediately sent him the insurance information and looked up the names and addresses of a few dentists near the college. Weeks went by and we hadn't heard from him. Cheri and I sent him a text every few days just checking in to see how he was doing, wondering if he ever went to the dentist. Nothing. Neither one of us heard back from him. Two months later, I received a text from an unknown number. The text read, "Hey, Dad, it's Matt. I borrowed someone's phone to let you know my cell phone was turned off. Can you help me out?" I immediately called the cellular provider and was able to get his phone turned on again. I did this because if I didn't, I may never hear from him.

Another two months went by, and Cheri and I heard nothing from him. We knew the phone was working because we called the cellular provider. We finally heard from him a few weeks later and this time he was in tears and his voice broken. He said, "Dad, I'm in a really bad place. I don't have any money. I don't know where my next meal will come from. I don't even know if I have a place to sleep tonight." Cheri and I were heartbroken over this news, so we transferred money to his account so he could eat and had some money for a place to stay until he got back home for Christmas.

When he arrived home for Christmas, we had a long talk with him—a face-to-face, heart-to-heart discussion about what was happening in his life. We discussed what his plans were and what may have gone wrong. Having this face-to-face discussion, this heart-to-heart, was not what our son wanted, because it was convicting. It was difficult. It was uncomfortable. And he knew that Cheri and I were disappointed with his choices. But it brought us closer together. We didn't love him any less because he messed up. We all mess up! We just wanted him to talk to us, to share his life, his accomplishments, and even his failures with us. Us sending him money and health insurance information is not a real relationship, but sitting down and talking together is.

Some of us treat God the exact same way our son treated Cheri and me. We don't talk to God. We don't share our failures; we try to work through them on our own. We don't share our successes with God; we take credit for them instead. We probably only pray to Him when we want something. We throw up that quick, 30-second microwave prayer asking God to help us say the right thing during an interview or asking Him to help out our finances when all else fails. That is not what God wants from us; that is not a relationship. That is where I was during my first marriage. That is why I didn't have peace or joy. The Holy Spirit is power, and

I wasn't tapping into that power. I didn't fuel my power source through worship or the Word of God, so was it any wonder I had conflict with others? That I was disappointed and frustrated with others? I was falling for the tricks of the devil; the knowledge of good and evil made me like a god (Gen. 3:5), so I didn't think I needed God in my life. In my pride, I thought I could do everything in my own power.

That is not how God intended it to work. Christ knew that, and it's why he got down on his knees and worshipped God in the Spirit. In the gospels, there are dozens of references to Christ praying. He prayed for others (Matt. 19:13). He prayed with others (Luke 9:28). He prayed alone (Luke 5:16, Matt 26:36-44). He prayed long prayers and short prayers (Luke 6:12, 18:1). He prayed heartfelt prayers regularly, and he taught others to pray (Matt. 6:9–13; John 4:24). There are many more verses on prayer in the gospels, but know that Jesus prayed all the time.

When we follow Jesus's example and are constantly in prayer, then we are filled with the Spirit, and we walk in the Holy Spirit. The two greatest commandments are to love God and love others:

Matthew 22:37–39 – 37Jesus said unto him, Thou shalt love the Lord thy God with all thy heart, and with all thy soul, and with all thy mind. 38This is the first and great commandment. 39And the second is like unto it, Thou shalt love thy neighbour as thyself.

When we are worshipping God and when we are spending time in a relationship with him above all else, we are following the first commandment. Then the second commandment is acting out God's will by loving others and meeting their needs above our own. The devil tries to get us to focus on us. It's all about what I want to have, what I want to be, and what I want to do. When we act like that, the devil is attacking, and he is winning.

The Need for Joy

The spiritual need for joy comes from fulfilling God's will in our lives by serving others.

> *1 Peter 4:13 – But rejoice, inasmuch as ye are partakers of Christ's sufferings; that, when his glory shall be revealed, ye may be glad also with exceeding joy.*

Putting your own needs aside and bearing the burden for others means to bear a cross. When you pick up your cross for one of God's children, you will have joy. Let's look at an example from the book of Ecclesiastes of a man who had all the temptations of the flesh:

> *Ecclesiastes 2:4–11 4I made me great works; I builded me houses; I planted me vineyards: 5I made me gardens and orchards, and I planted trees in them of all kind of fruits: 6I made me pools of water, to water therewith the wood that bringeth forth trees: 7I got me servants and maidens, and had servants born in my house; also I had great possessions of great and small cattle above all that were in Jerusalem before me: 8I gathered me also silver and gold, and the peculiar treasure of kings and of the provinces: I gat me men singers and women singers, and the delights of the sons of men, as musical instruments, and that of all sorts. 9So I was great, and increased more than all that were before me in Jerusalem: also my wisdom remained with me. 10And whatsoever mine eyes desired I kept not from them, I withheld not my heart from any joy; for my heart rejoiced in all my labour: and this was my portion of all my labour. 11Then I looked on all the works that my hands had wrought, and on the labour that I had laboured to do: and, behold, all was vanity and vexation of spirit, and there was no profit under the sun.*

Whatever Solomon saw, he wanted—the lust of the eyes. He had great works (v. 4) and great possessions (v. 7). He had big houses and fancy gardens with a pool and all kinds of fruit (vv. 4–6). He had servants to attend to all his needs (v. 7). He had silver, gold, and treasures, and he had entertainment (v. 8). Whatever Solomon wanted, he possessed.

He also had the pride of life. He believed he was better than anyone else because he was the king:

> *Ecclesiastes 2:9 – I was great, and increased more than all that were before me in Jerusalem:*

Solomon had the lust of the flesh. He did whatever he wanted:

> *Ecclesiastes 2:10 – ...I withheld not my heart from any joy*

Solomon had it all, he did it all, and he was the greatest of all. But then look what he realized in verse 11:

> *Ecclesiastes 2:11 – ...all was vanity and vexation of Spirit*

Vanity means useless or empty. He called all those things pointless and no good. All the money to buy whatever he wanted to have, the ability to do whatever he wanted to do, and the ability to be whatever he wanted to be—he called it all vanity. He also said it was a vexation to his spirit. All that he had, everything this world had to offer, was troublesome to his spirit.

The reason the temptations of this world are useless and troublesome to our spirits is because the world is opposed to the Spirit. Solomon gathered all and did it all, and wanted it all for himself. Look again at the underlined text about Solomon:

> [4]***I made me*** *great works;* ***I builded me*** *houses;* ***I planted me*** *vineyards:* [5] ***I made me*** *gardens and orchards, and I planted trees in them of all kind of fruits:* [6] ***I made me*** *pools of water, to water therewith the wood that bringeth forth trees:* [7] ***I got me*** *servants and maidens, and had servants born** in my house**; also I had great possessions of great and small cattle above all that were in Jerusalem before **me:*** [8] ***I gathered me*** *also silver and gold, and the peculiar treasure of kings and of the provinces**: I gat me** men singers and women singers, and the delights of the sons of men, as musical instruments, and that of all sorts.* [9] *So* ***I was great,***

60

*and **increased more than all** that were before me in Jerusalem: also my wisdom remained with me. [10] And whatsoever **mine** eyes desired I kept not from them, **I withheld not my heart from any joy;** for my heart rejoiced in all my labour: and this was my portion of all my labour. [11] Then I looked on all the works that my hands had wrought, and on the labour that I had laboured to do: and, behold, **all was vanity and vexation of spirit, and there was no profit under the sun**.*

Everything Solomon ever did was for himself. No wonder it was useless. No wonder it didn't bring him joy but brought him worry and trouble. Perhaps if these words said, "I made something for others, I built for others, I planted for others, and I gathered for others," then it would have been joy to his soul and fullness of spirit. I can personally tell you that nothing brings me greater joy than to be a servant to others, to be used of God to bless other people. I don't get joy-filled when I sit on the sofa and binge watch TV; that is what the devil tells me to do, and that is what my flesh might entice me to do. The flesh says focus on yourself, but that doesn't help grow strong relationships.

Filling our spirit with God's love and then giving that love away to other people by doing God's will creates joy. When we have the heart to put other's needs before our own, especially in our marriages, we will have joy and a joy-filled marriage.

A few years ago, my wife was feeling down because she didn't feel she had any true friends. We just assumed it was because we had gotten older and was distracted by raising our kids and working the nine-to-five grind. We started attending our church's Friday night program, where we met people who had needs that surpassed our imagination. They truly did need a friend, someone to listen to them, someone to cry with, and someone to show them godly love. We both began to grow a bond with these new friends. By showing them love, they gave love in return. We grew closer to the Friday night church members and the staff. We yielded to the Holy Spirit by putting other's needs before our own. Sure, we would have liked to have snuggled on the couch every Friday in our pajamas, ordered take-out, and binge watched something on the DVR, but what kind of lasting joy would that have brought us? We figured out that finding joy is about serving others and doing God's will to be a blessing to others.

When my wife turned 50 years old, I asked her what she wanted to do to celebrate. She wanted her friends to come over and just spend time with her. Do you know that we had over 90 people in our house that night?! The year before I would have struggled to fill the living room. She is more filled with joy, and she has more true friends now who would be there for her when she needs them. Why? Because she understands love is meeting the needs of others and putting her own wants and needs aside. She does that in God's power, fueled by the Holy Spirit. She has taken on the form of a servant to please others.

John 15:13 – Greater love hath no man than this, that a man lay down his life for his friends.

Because Cheri was meeting their needs, they wanted to meet hers. They enjoyed being around her and couldn't wait to be there for her. What changed? How did my wife go from feeling lonely and without friends to feeling so very loved? Cheri was acting more like Jesus Christ, and everyone wants to be around the light of Jesus! Ninety people were there for her. Ninety people came to support her because she adopted the mind of Christ, took on the form of a servant, and laid down her life for others, just like Jesus Christ (Phil. 2:1–7). By giving herself away, she gained even more.

1 Corinthians 9:19 – …yet have I made myself servant unto all, that I might gain the more.

Let's revisit the verse that started this chapter:

Romans 15:13 – Now the God of hope fill you with all joy and peace in believing, that ye may abound in hope, through the power of the Holy Ghost.

All of our spiritual needs are met when we allow God to fill us. By believing and trusting in God's promises, we can abound in hope. These spiritual needs come from God and godly living.

RELATIONAL NEEDS

The quality of our lives is equivalent to the quality of our relationships. There have been studies done to measure happiness among the secular world, and the results may surprise you. The root of happiness is based on the quality of our relationships more than any other factor. Happiness is not the money we make, the car we drive, or the job we have. Our happiness is based on the quality of our relationships. There are many people that have experienced loss of their house in a fire, loss of their wealth through poor investments, or the loss of a job. In all those circumstances, the person was most likely extremely distressed and troubled, but that didn't compare to the loss of a loved one. Even Solomon penned the following about relationships:

> *Ecclesiastes 4:9–10 – Two are better than one; because they have a good return for their labour. For if they fall, the one will lift up his fellow: but woe to him that is alone when he falleth; for he hath not another to lift him up.*

The reality is that not all relationships are of good quality. What makes one relationship higher quality than another? It's based on the amount of love we receive from those relationships. Love is action, where another person meets our needs expecting nothing in return. If we feel loved when someone meets our needs, then a high-quality relationship is when many more needs are being met on a consistent basis. There are six needs that must be met in every relationship:

- Trust
- Encouragement
- Gratitude
- Acceptance
- Understanding
- Forgiveness

Each of these needs exist in every relationships to varying degrees. The more often you meet these needs in a relationship, the stronger the relationship will become. The higher the quality of your relationships the happier you are because your friends trust, encourage, gratitude, accept, understand, and forgive you.

THE NEED FOR TRUST

Trust is the most critical component of a good relationship and is the basis for our love feeling. The best way to explain the need of trust is to share a situation I encountered a long time ago. I once was friends with a guy who always had a smile on his face; he was always happy to see me and would say, "HEY! It's great to see you!" I loved it! I felt so accepted and warm around him. Over time, our friendship grew, and I would see him say the same thing to other people. The difference was, as soon as we were alone, he would say things like "She is too big to be wearing something like that," or "Can you believe that guy bought a new car? He is in debt up to his eyeballs." I found myself wondering, *Does he makes comments like that behind my back?* Face to face, he appeared accepting and genuine, but as I learned more about him, I saw he was hypocritical and insincere. His smile stopped having a positive effect on me as I no longer believed he was genuine. Was he ever really happy to see me? If the sincerity of the message is in doubt, then the loving action doesn't produce a loving feeling. If someone is trying to meet a need but they aren't trustworthy, we will doubt their sincerity. So were they actually meeting the need of trust to begin with?

When our oldest son went off to college, he would call regularly at first. As time progressed, the calls would be less and less frequent until it got to the point that the only time I heard from him was when he wanted something. "Dad, I need more money," "Dad, I need the insurance card," or "Dad, I need..." After a few months of this behavior, when he did call, I had the urge to answer the phone, "Yeah, what do you want this time?" but I didn't. I loved hearing my son say, "I love you" and "I miss you," but those words sounded insincere and didn't mean as much as they used to mean when "I need" was attached to them.

Trust is built over time. It takes a long time to build up trust but only one moment or one action to lose it all. It's a repetitive process of validating the character and the integrity of the person. Trust is the assurance of a future behavior. When we apply for a loan, the bank will pull our credit scores. There are very smart people that have isolated key attributes to predict behavior (e.g., paying our bills on time, debt to income ratio, etc.) and have boiled it down into a score. These attributes represent risk. I will pay more for my car insurance if I am a bigger risk and if there is lack of trust in my ability to drive without causing an accident. Like our credit score, trust is based on the predictability of a behavior.

In relationships, in order to build trust, we must take a risk. A single person looking for their future spouse has to take a risk by asking someone on a date. Exposing yourself to new things and new people is where we take risks. While dating, you could eventually make yourself vulnerable to the point of getting hurt. As the dating relationship grows, you share more about your past, your dreams, and your innermost thoughts. If the person you are dating doesn't share this with others, then trust is built. You need to take a risk by exposing yourself to possibly being hurt in order to build trust.

Trust comes after good results happen. Consistent behavior that becomes predictable builds trust. As this trust builds, we start to have closer relationships. Below I have defined five types of relationships that reflect this phenomenon:

- Stranger – As a stranger, your trust level is nonexistent. You haven't built any trust with them because there is no basis for that trust. There is no past history or behavior, because we don't know them.

- Acquaintance – An acquaintance is someone that is known but that is not a close friend. This is a person that you know very little about. It includes people that you associate with at work, around the neighborhood, or in some other social group. You have one or two things in common with them. Perhaps you work in the same place and both have school-age children but really don't know one another. Your trust level with an acquaintance is low. Another example of an acquaintance could be someone from church; you may or may not remember their name, and you don't necessarily associate with one another outside of church.

- Friends – Friends are people that you like and enjoy being with, a person that helps or supports someone or something (such as a cause). The trust level here is medium. I may trust them enough to loan them $20 with expectation of repayment, but I probably don't associate with them closely enough to witness their behavior to trust them with larger amounts of money, to watch my children for a short period of time, or even borrow something of value (e.g., my car).

- Companion – A companion or good friend is someone to whom you feel closely connected, someone you spend lots of time with. The trust level is typically high because you have more exposure to their ongoing behavior. You know the consistency of their character through actions and stories they have shared. On average, people will have two to five best friends or companions. Much energy and time are spent in these relationships, sharing stories and sharing decisions and thought processes. We invest time in cultivating and working on these relationships. Typically, the more we have in common with someone, the more we think and act like them, the more we accept them, and the more we want to be around them. We have a high tolerance and are quick to forgive these friends. Mutual respect and sacrifice are common among these types of good friends.

- Spouse – This should be the strongest type of relationship. This is when two or more people work toward a common goal. They know one another extremely well and have had lots of time to observe their character, past behavior, and actions in order to have complete trust in one another. A marital relationship shares a home, finances, and decisions of life and death with one another.

Perhaps these deep relationships started with some loving actions that built trust. Through consistent positive behavior, repaying a small loan, returning something borrowed, and being there for them in a time of need, your loving actions built the expectation of predictable results, thus increasing trust and a feeling of closeness.

Trust is foundational in any relationship, which is the reason I began this section with the need of trust. Without trust, there is no relationship. Period. Part of dating is to move from friends to building a complete trust with someone. That is why breeches of trust in a marriage (e.g., infidelity) are so devastating. When we are married, we put complete trust in our spouse, and when that trust is broken, it is difficult if not impossible to rebuild.

If I say the right thing but people don't believe it or trust it, it becomes meaningless. Have you ever walked past someone at work and they say, "Hi, how are you today?" and you try to answer them but they keep walking, not waiting to hear your answer? Did they really care how you were doing? Was it just going through the motions of what we were taught to say and do? Doesn't trust build when that same person who said hi and asked how you were doing actually pauses and listens to your answer? You now trust they are being sincere and are showing a real interest in you. We can fool some of our acquaintances, friends, or even our spouse some of the time, but eventually they will figure out if we are sincere or not. Trust is the foundation of any relationship; it comes before love and is essential to marriage.

What happened first for you, your love for Christ or your trust in Christ? We need to trust Jesus first before we are saved. Christ loved us and died for us, and we must first trust (or believe) in that action for eternal salvation before love can be in our hearts.

Romans 10:9 – That if thou shalt confess with thy mouth the Lord Jesus, and shalt believe in thine heart that God hath raised him from the dead, thou shalt be saved.

The Bible says, "*Believe* in thine heart." To believe implies to trust in Jesus. This verse doesn't focus on loving God. Love or closeness comes when loving needs are met. When our friends, companions, or spouse show loving actions that meet our needs, loving feelings follow. We love Him because he first loved us (1 John 4:19). God showed his love toward us that while we were yet sinners, he sent his Son to die for us (Romans 5:8). His Son, Jesus Christ, took on our sins, and because of that, God was able to show us mercy, grace, and forgiveness. That is why we love him.

When we are trying to build closeness with people over time, we see their actions, study their actions, and investigate their actions before we believe and truly trust that the actions are genuine. Trust is where relationships begin.

It's the same with God. We put our trust in God because his character is unchangeable, and as a saved Christian, you have seen evidence of his loving actions toward you. When I married Cheri, we said the words "as long as we both shall live, I promise," and we began our relationship and our marriage with trust.

Cheri and I started out as work acquaintances. We were assigned to work on projects together and relied on one another to be successful at work. This is how we first started building trust. We both were diligent workers: We made sure to meet deadlines, were respectful of each other's time, and worked well as a team. After some months of working together, we began to engage in social activities with other work friends. We got to know one another outside of work on a more social level, where we talked about politics, religion, family, and many other topics.

Trust was building. We began to personally confide in one another. We talked about our pasts and shared about how we had made bad decisions and the consequences from those decisions. We didn't judge one another or betray the confidential things we shared with one another. By keeping those personal details private, we built even more trust in each other. As we spent more time together, we realized we had more and more in common, and we grew closer to each other. Soon we started planning times when our kids could play together. We even allowed each other to watch our children for small periods of time. After more than a year, we began dating one another, spending time one on one and sharing more intimate details of our lives as we shared more and more of our time together. Before I asked Cheri to marry me, we had built such a close relationship that she was my best friend, my confidant. Our trust was complete. I would have trusted her with anything, including my children or my finances.

Conversely, my ex-wife had substantial debt before our marriage. I trusted her in a lot of ways, but I didn't in the area of finances. Even in our marriage, we had separate bank accounts. Our relationship never worked because it never reached the level of complete trust. There are many additional reasons our relationship failed, but a lack of trust will erode the foundation or never allow it to be built at all.

Dating and Trust

Dating is a time to validate the character of your potential spouse. We can only judge people by their words and actions. Therefore, communication and observation will be essential while dating. As we try to build trust, it is absolutely critical for us to be honest and open. Giving someone uninterrupted attention and sharing your thoughts, feelings, experiences, and dreams with them creates a bond. Being honest and not leaving out information prevents them from filling in the gaps with what they think is the truth, which creates suspicion. The best way to prevent someone from being suspicious is to over communicate. Even if you think they know the answer or the truth, you should state it so there is no doubt.

I'm not saying we need to bare our soul on the first date, but if and when we consider this person to be a potential spouse, we will need to focus on good communication. We need to sit together with no distractions and seriously talk and answer each other's questions honestly while sharing thoughts and feelings openly. Don't be discouraged over disagreements. I don't know a single couple on the same page about everything. It's good to talk through these differences of opinion and understand where you and your potential spouse differ. Through this experience, potential spouses can learn about one another and truly decide if this is the person they should marry.

You should also observe your potential spouse to validate their character. With careful observation, the true content of our character will eventually show itself. Perhaps the person you're dating is really nice, considerate, and caring toward you, but how do they speak about other people? How do they treat the hostess at a restaurant or complete strangers in need? We can put our best foot forward most times, but eventually the truth will come out. See how that person treats their co-workers, parents, siblings, authority figures, and neighbors. Do they go out of their way for others or only think of themselves?

They may tell you they are really passionate about something, but their actions may not validate their words. For this reason, dating for an extended duration is always advisable. While dating, people will typically put their best foot forward. Guys will buy new clothes, tuck in their shirts, and wear cologne. Ladies will put on make-up, do their hair, and get their nails done. Most will suddenly watch what they eat and start working out. We naturally try to hide the warts of our imperfections, but the ultimate goal of dating is to validate the true character of a potential spouse.

In my first marriage, I not only rushed into the relationship but I rushed into the marriage too. In hindsight, I saw actions that were indicators of future problems, but I believed the lie of the devil that no matter what the issue, we could overcome it if we just loved each other.

Six weeks after Cheri met her first husband, she moved in with him. She couldn't see past the loving emotions she felt when she was with him. He needed a roommate to help with the cost of a new condo, and she wanted to move out of her parents' house and be independent. They enjoyed spending time together, so in their eyes, this was a win–win! In hindsight, she should have seen this desperate attempt to manage money as a potential problem that might plague them later in their marriage, and it did…but more on that later.

Learning from our pasts, Cheri and I took things slowly. With the slightest hint of an issue with either of us, we started probing, having deep, meaningful conversations as we took the time to validate those words through actions. When I first met Cheri, she attended a different church but wasn't a saved Christian. I remember one Saturday night we were having dinner together, and I mentioned that I was excited to go to church in the morning. She looked at me with shock. She thought church was something you were obligated to do and didn't understand it was about having a personal relationship with Jesus Christ. In order for her to be a prospect for dating and potential marriage, she needed to be a saved Christian, so I invited her to church with me. She was initially overwhelmed and wasn't that excited about it; however, through our ongoing conversations, I could tell her mind was still open. She visited our church on and off over a six-month period until she eventually was as excited as I was to go. A few weeks later, she was saved, and I saw a significant difference in her. She prayed more, she talked about God more, and she seemed more at peace. We had long conversations centered around God. She would ask me questions, and we would study the answer together. We began to go to church activities together. Not only did she profess to love God but I could see it in her actions too.

It takes time and perseverance to establish a relationship built on trust, but those strong relationships are worth the effort. I find it astounding when people tell me that within two to three months they moved their relationship from strangers or acquaintances to wanting to get married. How can you possibly know someone's true character after such a short amount of time? There is no time to validate behavior. If we don't take things slowly in our relationships, we may overlook those warning signs that indicate a friend truly isn't our friend at all.

Growing a relationship from stranger to spouse should not happen in a matter of weeks. If you want a marriage that will last, you should marry your best friend—someone who does things for you not because of what they may receive in return but because they truly care about you.

Building trust during dating is based on two factors: honesty and transparency.

1. Building Trust: Honesty
First and foremost, trust is built on honesty:

> *James 5:12 – But above all things, my brethren, swear not, neither by heaven, neither by the earth, neither by any other*

oath: but let your yea be yea; and your nay, nay; lest ye fall into
condemnation.

Our words and actions indicate reliability. James 5 says to let your no be no and your yes be yes. As I mentioned, trust is built on past actions and predictable results. We call that a reputation. Reputation is our report card of perceived reliability. Every friend has a report card on you.

When you are dishonest or unreliable, friendships will erode. Let's do a self-examination: Do you fudge the numbers on your taxes? Do you go to amusement parks and tell your kids to pretend they are younger than they are to get them in at a cheaper rate?

One summer I took my kids to Hershey Park. Ryan was six, and Matthew was 11. The tickets were $15 less for children ages three to nine. After spending $10 for parking and knowing I was about to spend an exorbitant amount of money on food, locker rentals, and carnival games, I justified saving an extra $15 by ordering two children's tickets and one adult ticket. As I made the order, Matthew spoke out, "but, Dad, I'm 11!" I didn't even think my boys were paying attention. After the ticket vendor gave me a glare, I promptly said two adults and one child. I've always told my boys I would never lie to them, that I would always tell them the truth, but how could they believe that when I had just lied to someone else right in front of them? Was my integrity really worth saving $15? I learned an important lesson that day. I can lie to strangers and justify my poor behavior, but it's not worth undermining the trust in my close relationships.

People that matter to us know who we really are. The ones who don't know us might be fooled at first, but when it's finally exposed, the damage you do to your integrity will hurt your reputation.

1 Timothy 1:5 – ...charity out of a pure heart, and of a good
conscience, and of faith unfeigned:

Unfeigned means real or without hypocrisy.[4] Our charity (loving

---

4 http://webstersdictionary1828.com/Dictionary/Unfeigned

actions), good conscience, and faith should be real. I have faults, and I'm not perfect; I am no longer hiding that fact. My spouse, my children, and my close friends want me to be real, not perfect. The more people see us acting without integrity, the more they will doubt our honesty, which will affect our reputation.

2. Building Trust: Transparency

Transparency is the second basis of trust. Are you afraid to share something about yourself to the one you're dating because you may lose the relationship?

> *Ephesians 4:25 — Wherefore putting away lying, speak every man truth with his neighbour: for we are members one of another.*

If we really believe that the person we are dating could be a potential spouse, then we need to be open and honest. We need to start opening the book about our past, where we go, what we do, and who we hang out with. Don't be ambiguous about where you are going. If someone you hope to grow closer to asks where you are going, your answer should be the entire truth; don't leave pieces out. We need to be transparent. If you are the one asking and you are getting partial answers, that should be an indicator that the person may be hiding something.

In dating relationships, as we grow closer together, we should be revealing more about ourselves. On that first date, we tend to make sure all of our flaws are hidden so we can impress them enough for a second date. As date #2 turns into date #3 and so on, they will begin to see us not quite at our best. Guys that were once ironing their shirt for date #1 are now throwing it back in the dryer for date #6 just to get some of the bad wrinkles out. Ladies may decide they don't need to have pristine nails and hair by date #10. As the dates progress, we are starting to show not only our true outer appearance but also our inner self. This is what should be transpiring during dating.

Being transparent is when we expose *all of ourselves* to our prospective spouse, not hide it. Perhaps you don't like to cook but your first date is a home-cooked meal, perhaps you hate to clean but your house is maintained immaculately when dating, or perhaps you work out all the time when you're really a couch potato. The problem is when you get married and revert back to your normal self, it becomes a shock to your new spouse because you never revealed your true self while dating.

Perhaps you have this deep, dark secret you think no one will ever forgive. When it comes out *after* marriage, it disrupts the foundation of that marriage. It is absolutely essential that you expose 100% of who you really are and were before you are married so that when you promise to fulfill those vows, they are based on a sturdy foundation.

When Cheri and I first became friends, we began to share some details of our pasts with one another. We both felt comfortable doing so, even before the dating began. We shared our pasts that neither one of was very proud of regarding past relationships and poor decisions and the consequences we faced because of those decisions. We shared details about our jobs and where we may have failed, our financial struggles and where we went wrong, and the current struggles we were still fighting. Being this transparent built trust over time. It took more than two years for our relationship to evolve into total trust (honesty and transparency).

After marriage, when two are one flesh, there shouldn't be any surprises. Your spouse should have all of your passwords (accounts, cell phone, email, social media), and your search history should be open and available. If your spouse asks to look at it, let them look at it. When married, passwords become unnecessary with each other. You should have one social media account (Facebook, Instagram, Twitter), onc email, and one bank account. If you both agree to keep separate accounts (which we don't recommend), then make sure your spouse has access to anything they want when they want. You are one flesh and one body.

Mark 10:8 – And they twain shall be one flesh: so then they are no more twain, but one flesh.

THE NEED FOR ENCOURAGEMENT

We all need encouragement. Life is hard, and we can get discouraged with major issues such as a bad health report, job loss, or disobedient kids. We can also become discouraged during day-to-day life. When life gets us down, keeping our focus on Jesus Christ will allow us to persevere even in the toughest of times. The Bible tells us the following:

> *Psalm 9:9 – The LORD also will be a refuge for the oppressed, a refuge in times of trouble.*

> *Psalm 23:4 – Yea, though I walk through the valley of the shadow of death, I will fear no evil: for thou art with me; thy rod and thy staff they comfort me*

> *Romans 8:6 – For to be carnally minded is death; but to be spiritually minded is life and peace.*

These verses indicate that God is with us through good times and bad times. He will support us and give us peace during our trials and tribulations. Not only did God promise to be a comfort to us in troubled times but he also put other Christians in our lives to help encourage us every day. The Bible instructs fellow believers to encourage those around us:

> *1 Thessalonians 5:11 – Wherefore comfort yourselves together, and edify one another, even as also ye do.*

This passage tells us to comfort others and edify, or build up, other Christian believers. God places Christians in our lives with a diverse set of backgrounds and experiences so that we can help one another through those rough experiences. There is nothing you have been through in your life that hasn't afflicted someone else. When we are going through a dark valley, our friends can help us see the light at the end of the tunnel. We all need a friend who can lift us up, who can bolster our spirits with words of encouragement. As we grow a relationship from friend to spouse, we should be looking for someone that is an encouragement to us, someone who can build us up. Spouses should encourage each other. Many times in my marriage to Cheri, she has helped me navigate a tribulation by being supportive, by listening, by helping me to focus on the positive, or by helping me to come up with a plan to overcome the struggle.

This is the example of Jesus Christ that we show one another in our marriage. We make each other feel wanted and supported, and we always have each other's back. We endure trials <u>together</u>, uplift one another when we are down, and are fierce advocates for one another. We show each other compassion by praying together, calling one another in the middle of the day just to say, "I love you," and greeting one another after a long day with open arms, a hug, and a smile that just makes the troubles of the world disappear long enough to give us hope to keep going. The world can be a cruel, dark place that will get us down if we let it, but our spouses should be able to be a light in this dark world that will lift our spirits.

Studies show negative emotions can adversely impact our decision making, make us pessimistic, decrease cognitive processing, inhibit our immune system, and impair our concentration, while positive emotions make us optimistic and hopeful, increase our cognitive processing, improve our immune system, and help us better focus.[5],[6] The Bible is riddled with stories of disappointment, tribulation, affliction, provocation, and persecution that can lead to negative emotions of fear, depression, and anger. In isolation, our negativity can easily consume our thoughts.

Cheri never had a serious boyfriend in high school. She went on dates occasionally, but nothing ever lasted very long. She was preoccupied with other interests besides boys, and most guys viewed her as more of a friend than a dating prospect. But in her

---

5 Study published in *Psychotherapy and Psychosomatics* (Vol 72, p253)
6 *Emotion and Decision Making* by Learner, Yi, Vladesolo, Kassam (16 June 2014)

senior year, she met someone who made her feel special. She loved to hang around with him, and she started to have feelings for him. Throughout the year, they would do things together, usually in a group setting. Later that year, he asked her to the prom. She was ecstatic! Finally a boy was interested in her, and he was funny and attractive and really understood her. For weeks leading up to the prom, she was so happy. They had a great time together that night, including a kiss at the end of the night. But that kiss was on the cheek, and he said, "I'm so glad I went to the dance with one of my best friends." She could barely get inside her house before the tears came running down her face. She thought this relationship meant so much more. How could she be so stupid? How could she face him again the next day at school without welling up with tears?

The following year she graduated and started college, where she did meet her first serious boyfriend. The happiest moments were when the two of them were together. They talked on the phone every day, and it was amazing. However, like all relationships, when the dilapidation phase began and the calls became less frequent, Cheri's happiness was up and down. The days when he called and she saw him were "great" days, and the days when he didn't call or she couldn't see him were "awful" days. She based her life on her circumstances. On those good days, she did well in school, she had a smile on her face, and she was upbeat and radiant. On those bad days, she was upset, irritable, unable to concentrate in school, and sometimes depressed.

God will sometimes use those times to draw us close to him and help us grow as Christians:

Romans 5:1–5 — ¹Therefore being justified by faith, we have peace with God through our Lord Jesus Christ: ²By whom also we have access by faith into this grace wherein we stand, and rejoice in hope of the glory of God. ³And not only so, but we glory in tribulations also: knowing that tribulation worketh patience; ⁴And patience, experience; and experience, hope: ⁵And hope maketh not ashamed; because the love of God is shed abroad in our hearts by the Holy Ghost which is given unto us.

This passage tells us that Jesus gives us peace with God and that because of that peace, we are in God's grace and therefore should have hope in all circumstances, good or bad. In other words, God loves us and won't allow bad things to happen to us unless there is a "good reason."

God will use bad circumstances to do good things. This is why verse 3 tells us to "glory in tribulation"—because God is making these bad things work together for a good purpose (Rom. 8:28). That purpose is patience, experience, and hope (vv. 3–4).

Christian maturity comes through trials in our lives. Verse 4 calls it experience. When hard times come and we sit back patiently and allow God to work in our lives, good results eventually are produced. These good results increase our faith in God, which also increases our hope in God. We become more reliant on God and more trusting in God, and therefore greater peace is produced in our lives.

That happy/sad roller coaster of a relationship that Cheri had with her first boyfriend finally came to an end after five years. Cheri's self-confidence was at a low point. She met her first husband, and 10 years later, they divorced. It wasn't until she was faced with yet another heartbreak and another life-changing trial that she sought God. Before God was in her life and before she trusted him, bad circumstances produced negative emotions, which resulted in stress, depression, or anger. Today negative circumstances still make her upset at first (after all, no one likes trials!), but she bounces back the moment she talks to God and realizes that God has something better in store. Today Cheri has a better understanding of the benefits of remaining positive:

Job 6:8–10 – ⁸Oh that I might have my request; and that God would grant me the thing that I long for! ⁹Even that it would please God to destroy me; that he would let loose his hand, and cut me off! ¹⁰Then should I yet have comfort; yea, I would harden myself in sorrow: let him not spare; for I have not concealed the words of the Holy One.

In chapter 6 of Job, Job was in a great despair; he had lost everything: his children, his land, his cattle, etc. It was so bad that he asked God to take his life, to "destroy" him. In verse 10, he said that death would bring him comfort. However, despite all the heartache, somehow Job knew God had his plan and that all things were eventually going to work together for good. In the midst of all his pain, he knew God was trying to teach him something:

Job 6:24 – Teach me, and I will hold my tongue: and cause me to understand wherein I have erred.

Jesus will allow us to persevere even in the toughest of times. Jesus himself cannot reach down and touch us, so he uses others to do it for him. God puts fellow Christians in our lives to help us through tough times. We all need that friend that can lift us up, that can bolster our spirits with a smile and a hug or words of encouragement. When we are going through a dark valley, our friends can help us see the light at the end of the tunnel.

Christ promises to comfort those who belong to him:

John 14:18 – I will not leave you comfortless: I will come to you.

He does this by influencing fellow believers through the Holy Spirit. The Bible instructs us to comfort others but to exhort others too (2 Tim. 4:2). Exhortation is to embolden, cheer, or advise. Primary sense is to give strength and courage[7]. There are many people that offer comfort and exhortation in the bible including John the Baptist (Luke 3:18), Peter (Acts 2:40), and Barnabas (Acts 11:23). These men would make those that felt downhearted hopeful by offering comfort from God's Word without being judgmental.

2 Timothy 4:2 – Preach the word; be instant in season, out of season; reprove, rebuke, exhort with all longsuffering and doctrine.

---

7 http://webstersdictionary1828.com/Dictionary/Exhort

Encouraging others requires us to be patient with the shortcomings of others. The Bible refers to this as longsuffering. When trying to encourage, remind others that life is a constant race—a marathon—and that we are always improving. We may not always win, and many times we fail, but that is how we improve. Learning from failure helps us to improve. We need to encourage others to keep running that race and to pick themselves off the ground—to cast off sins that are like weights that drag them down and keep them from finishing:

> *Hebrews 12:1 – Wherefore seeing we also are compassed about with so great a cloud of witnesses, let us lay aside every weight, and the sin which doth so easily beset us, and let us run with patience the race that is set before us,*

Our words should encourage others to use God for strength to finish the race. We ought to do everything in our power to encourage other believers in their walk with the Lord.

We need to praise others when they bear a hardship. If the hardship is self-inflicted and this person is turning to God and changing their life, that is to be commended. We should celebrate that with them. It will give them the strength to keep going.

There was a recent study done with two groups that were trying to lose weight. The groups were exactly the same in every way except that one group had received three encouraging text messages a week and the other received none. The group that received those encouraging texts lost, on average, 4.5 pounds more than the other group.[8] That is the power of encouraging words.

Our words and actions should help others to grow in their walk with the Lord:

> *Romans 14:19 – Let us therefore follow after the things which make for peace, and things wherewith one may edify another.*

---

8 https://www.mobihealthnews.com/26806/study-finds-text-messaging-effective-for-weight-loss/

Edify means to instruct and guide someone morally or intellectually.[9] When we talk to others, we need to edify them or help them to grow closer to Christ. Not only should our words encourage them but our actions should be an example that can motivate them to keep them from their sin and to put their faith in God. Some people, when life starts to get tough and trials come, will be discouraged, lose faith, and turn to worldly things for comfort. If we can be a potential comfort and encouragement to them, we can prevent the disastrous consequences of the world from destroying them.

God expects us to use our past tribulations or experiences (Rom. 5:3–4) to help others. Our church is full of people from all walks of life. We have a diverse set of backgrounds and experiences. There is nothing you have been through in your life that hasn't afflicted someone else as well. I'm sure if you ask around, there is someone at your local church to help you too.

Sometimes it's enough just to let people know that you've been where they are, you feel their pain, and you know they can survive this and ultimately be a better person too. There is a light at the other end of that dark tunnel, and if they just keep their focus on God, he will be faithful to produce good results from this bad experience.

Cheri and I used to teach a Sunday School class at Rosedale Baptist Church called New Beginnings; it was initially created to help people that were separated, divorced, or widowed. My wife and I felt God had called us to be a blessing to those people, to help them, to tell them we had been where they were and knew it seemed discouraging, but with God's grace and mercy, they would make it through this and would be a stronger Christian with a closer relationship to God. Teaching that class was a high point in our Christian walk. Cheri and I loved our ministry and loved being a blessing to others, so helping them in turn helped us too.

---

9 http://webstersdictionary1828.com/Dictionary/Edify

We all need people in our corner. Good relationships should have two people trying to encourage each other. We will be there for our friends who are hurting, we will say encouraging things about them in front of others, and we will help point them toward God with words and actions. When Job lost his children and his possessions, his friends came and sat with him in silence. Sometimes we don't need to say anything; we just need to be there for our friends, to pray with them and walk alongside them during their tough times.

Encouragement is a critical component to all relationships. We need to be there for our friends to comfort them when they are feeling down and to push them to seek Jesus in their times of trouble. Our spouse may not always know what we are going through, but they should encourage us, defend us, look at the bright side of our failings, and help us see our strengths, not focus on our weaknesses.

We may live in a world tainted by sin, a world of hurt and disappointments, but we have Jesus Christ comforting us, running alongside us in the form of our Christian friends to help comfort us through those dark times and to help us to be better people. The person we are married to or the person we want to be married to should run alongside of us and provide advice and comfort during our trials.

When a trial comes to our family, it's not fun, and I just want to fast forward to when we are done with it. Once we are through the trial, I realize that I'm a better version of myself. Most likely, while in a trial, we are spending more time talking to God and reading his Word, therefore I have been filled with the Holy Spirit, I'm more obedient to what God wants for me, and I'm better able to be used by God to be more of a comfort to others when they are dealing with a trial.

When it comes to dating and determining if they are the right one to marry, time will tell! We need to date our future spouses long enough to know that they will be there with us through those trials in our lives, that we can call on them when the going gets tough, and that they will encourage us to be better versions of our-selves by pointing us to the Lord during those trials in our lives.

THE NEED FOR GRATITUDE

Appreciation means to value or raise the value of. All relationships need the element of appreciation. The biblical word for apprecia-tion is honor. To honor something is to place a high value on it or to have a favorable opinion. The Bible tell us to "honor all men" (1 Peter 2:17). If we care about our friendships and marriages as we should, we will look for opportunities to show the other per-son how much we value them for who they are and what they do. This is gratitude. Gratitude is when we recognize the value in someone else.

Communion (also known as the Lord's Supper) is such a spe-cial time to a Christian. It is a way of remembering how valuable Jesus Christ is to us. It is a way to show our appreciation for his shedding his blood and breaking his body for us, which is our pathway to heaven (1 Cor 10:16–17).

Gratitude and appreciation are closely linked. Gratitude is an outward expression of the inner feeling of appreciation. We express gratitude to show how much we appreciate someone. Typically, we show gratitude immediately after someone does something to benefit us unexpectedly. When a stranger holds the door for me, I say thank you. When my wife cooks a delicious meal, I give her a compliment by telling her how great the meal tasted.

Appreciation can also be expressed on special days throughout the year, such as birthdays or anniversaries. A birthday celebration is a way to show someone that you appreciate or place high value on their life; that is why we celebrate that life. We also show we place high value on our marriage by celebrating anniversaries. We show our mothers and fathers, or the mother/father of our chil-dren, appreciation by celebrating Mother's Day or Father's Day. In our marriages, we need to take these opportunities to recognize the value of our spouse by expressing our appreciation on these special days of remembrance.

We need to show our spouses constant expressions of our gratitude. When our relationship is new during the infatuation phase, we tend to express gratitude often because everything is new and exciting, but over time, we have a tendency to take things for granted. If we aren't careful, we may be heading into that dilapidation phase that heads into trouble if not corrected. By failing to express our gratitude, we may begin a dilapidation in our marriage.

Taking time to express our appreciation for our spouse should be genuine and done on a daily basis. Annual events, such as birthdays and anniversaries, are important, but we should be constantly showing gratitude throughout the year, not just on special occasions. We need to make sure we are taking the proper effort and time to recognize how valuable our spouse is to us. When we forget, or don't place enough emphasis on birthdays or anniversaries, it is sending our spouse a very loud and clear message that we place more value on the things distracting us than we do on them or our marriage. When a big bill is due, like the annual property tax bill on my home, I know about it, I plan for it in advance, and I save money throughout the year. When a birthday or holiday comes along, we need to make sure we plan in the same way. We know it's coming; it happens the same day every year.

Cheri's birthday sometimes falls on Thanksgiving. Having a birthday on a holiday is tough because she may not get the attention and recognition that she deserves on her one special day. Back during her previous marriage, it was that day—her birthday *and* Thanksgiving. She got up at 7 a.m. to feed the baby, they played together in the living room, and she dressed him and got him ready for the day. It was now almost 11 a.m., so she woke up her husband and asked him to keep an eye on the baby so she could get in the shower. She waited to hear the words "Happy Birthday." Nothing. She assumed he just forgot because it was Thanksgiving Day. After getting a shower and getting dressed, she walked downstairs to where he was sitting with the baby. No "Happy Birthday." When they left for her parents', still no "Happy Birthday." They walked into her parents' house, and Cheri's dad and mom immediately greeted her with a giant hug and a "HAPPY BIRTHDAY!" Cheri glanced toward her husband, who had very little expression and didn't seem to be fazed. What Cheri didn't accept about him was that birthdays and holidays were never that important to him; therefore he didn't think they would be important to anyone else. He normally waited until the last minute to buy a gift or even the day of her birthday to say, "Hey let's go out and get you something nice." He didn't appreciate the symbolism of the birthday as a celebration of that person and all that they do throughout the year.

This was one of those stories that Cheri shared with me early on in our relationship. Cheri's parents always make a big deal about birthdays. Cheri also always makes a big deal about birthdays. I, too, like making a big deal about birthdays. I admit that I'm a bit of an oddball compared to my buddies (or so I've heard). I start shopping for Cheri's birthday and Christmas in August. I see something she would like, and I buy it. When her birthday falls on Thanksgiving, I typically go above and beyond other years. I have snuck out of the bedroom while she's sleeping to hang birthday signs and balloons and have left notes in the bathroom or on her steering wheel so that when she wakes up, she immediately knows that I appreciate her and that she is so very valuable to me.

Several studies have been performed to show the power of appreciation. A specific marriage study conducted by Dr. John Gottman and Robert Levenson observed couples' interactions and identified their interactions as either positive or negative. The results predicted that couples that made five positive comments to every one negative comment were more than likely going to have a successful marriage. In other words, more than 90% of those couples with less than the "magic ratio" of 5:1 ended in divorce within 10 years of the study.[10]

A study published in the *Harvard Business Review* evaluated positive employee feedback versus constructive criticism and found the most productive employees were the ones that received that same magic ratio of 5:1 positive feedback to negative.[11]

We all have the need to feel valued and appreciated in every relationship. Next to your relationship with God, your relationship with your spouse should be the most valuable relationship you have. Make sure you express your appreciation by showing your gratitude every day and on those special days throughout the year.

THE NEED FOR ACCEPTANCE

"In my opinion, the best thing you can do is find someone who loves you for exactly what you are. Good mood, bad mood, ugly, pretty, handsome, what have you." ~ Juno

Everyone has their oddities and will do things in their own way; no one is perfect. Before we get married, we should make sure we are able to accept and tolerate those imperfections and oddities in each other. If we don't accept people for who they are, their issues can turn into our annoyances. Those annoyances can be future sources of frustration.

When Cheri and I began dating, I noticed she was a woman who spoke her mind. We used to joke that she didn't have a filter. During the infatuation stage, I thought it was a positive attribute. I loved her honesty and her ability to stand up for herself. After we got married, I remember her dad saying to her, "Cheri, not everyone needs to know every thought in your head." I laughed out loud, and it hurt her feelings. You see, I thought she was able to

---

10 https://www.gottman.com/blog/the-magic-relationship-ratio-according-science
11 https://hbr.org/2013/03/the-ideal-praise-to-criticism

control her expressions but simply chose not to. When I laughed out loud at what her dad said and hurt her feelings, I thought she was just being too sensitive. What I didn't realize was that she felt rejected by me for laughing. After all, this was who she was. This had been her personality her entire life.

From that point on, over time, when I heard sermons on not being judgmental toward others, I learned how to better handle my wife's outward opinions. To do this, I needed to yield to the fruit of the Spirit when it came to longsuffering. Longsuffering is the ability to overlook faults in others without getting angry. Our goal in marriage is not to change the other person. God, through the Holy Spirit, will accomplish the change in our spouses. The only thing we are required to do is to love them:

> *Romans 15:1–7 – ¹We then that are strong ought to bear the infirmities of the weak, and not to please ourselves. ²Let every one of us please his neighbour for his good to edification. ³For even Christ pleased not himself; but, as it is written, The reproaches of them that reproached thee fell on me. ⁴For whatsoever things were written aforetime were written for our learning, that we through patience and comfort of the scriptures might have hope. ⁵Now the God of patience and consolation grant you to be likeminded one toward another according to Christ Jesus: ⁶That ye may with one mind and one mouth glorify God, even the Father of our Lord Jesus Christ. ⁷Wherefore receive ye one another, as Christ also received us to the glory of God.*

In Romans 15 above, verse 1 tells us that we need to bear, or support, the infirmities of the weak. When our brother or sister in Christ has struggled or failed, we need to be supportive. When my wife spoke out, it wasn't an excuse for me to get angry at her. I was not following God's commandments, and in turn, I was committing a sin against God by losing my temper. When we attack someone verbally, we are showing aggression against God; that doesn't make God happy nor will it help the situation you are dealing with.

In the latter half of verse 1 it says, "not to please ourselves." Isn't it gratifying to point out when someone frustrates us and doesn't do what we expect? Doesn't it feel good to let our disappointment and anger just fly out? This Bible verse says the stronger Christian should not give in to what the flesh wants by "telling them how it is." We should help to support the person with a different weakness than we have.

Verse 2 tells us to "please [our] neighbor for his good to edification." This means in order for someone to learn and change, we first need to accept them, not try to change them. In verse 7, it tells us to "receive (accept) ye one another." Why? Because Christ also accepted us. Christ didn't accept us *after* we got our act together; he accepted us when we were in bondage to our sin (Rom. 5:8). He accepted us when we were lost, and he accepted us when we were living in our sins from day to day. Once we accepted Jesus Christ, *then* he started changing us from the inside out. It's the job of the Christian (v. 2) to edify and the job of Holy Spirit to convict and change us. Edification isn't letting them have it, and it's not provoking them; it's loving them and accepting them and letting the Holy Spirit get a hold of them to change them.

The opposite of acceptance is rejection, and that isolated lonely feeling of being rejected can lead to poor physical and mental health. Everyone has the need to belong. Our churches should be safe havens for people to be who they are yet still feel a sense of belonging. If you are a member of a church, take the time to make others feel welcome and loved.

THE NEED FOR UNDERSTANDING

Offenses in life are going to come. Everyone reading this knows that they have been offended, upset, and angry over something someone did to them. Christ told his disciples in the Bible that it's impossible to avoid offenses:

Luke 17:1 – Then said he unto the disciples, It is impossible but that offences will come:

The world can be a cruel and harsh place, and if we don't properly handle our offenses, they will turn into bitterness that can destroy our relationships.

An offense comes as the result of a trespass. A trespass is when a boundary has been crossed, like when someone trespasses on your property and has physically crossed the boundary into your yard. A trespass can also be emotional. Have you ever heard the phrase "You just crossed the line"? When someone says that phrase, they are telling the other person they crossed their boundary of acceptable behavior. It's the feeling you get when you observe someone's behavior and say to yourself, "That was wrong. I would never do that."

All relationships, including marriages, will have offenses. Everyone is different, and our differences can be fascinating, but sometimes our differences can be irritating. Those irritating difference are sometimes called idiosyncrasies. An idiosyncrasy is defined as a "mode of behavior or way of thought peculiar to an individual." When we see someone do something peculiar, it can sometimes offend us because it's not the way we would behave.

In the section on acceptance, I mentioned that my wife speaks her mind quite frequently. She also has a habit of interrupting me. Cheri will blurt out thoughts in her head while I'm in the middle of talking. This habit was developed from childhood as the youngest of four girls. In a family of six, if you don't interrupt other people, you just don't get a chance to share your thoughts. I, on the other hand, have a tendency to be long-winded. I am very analytical and believe that exerting an opinion must come from the basis of fact; therefore, I tend to build up my points by providing long explanations for everything. Cheri's interruptions and my long-windedness are both idiosyncrasies. The problem is that Cheri can't wait for my long-winded explanations and will interrupt me. I've been offended on many occasions, and we have had arguments because I feel this is rude. Over the years of our marriage, I've learned to expect and accept this behavior from Cheri. At first I thought that by pointing out that her behavior was offensive, she would change. In fact, I got angrier every time she did it because she knew it offended me but did it anyway. What I have come to realize is that she doesn't do it on purpose but rather it's a habit established at childhood and one I don't think she will ever truly stop doing. She certainly does it less often than in the past. Now I view her restraint as a loving action toward me as opposed to her habitual idiosyncrasy as a purposeful act to hurt me. When she does interrupt me, she is more aware of it, and then she sees my restraint and not getting upset as a loving action toward her. This problem that used to cause conflict and distance between us is now something that draws us closer together. (And don't worry—Cheri has explained to me how my long-windedness bothers her, so I've made it a point to pick and choose those moments, and I try to be more to the point.)

That is why in the section on "The Need For Acceptance" we wrote, "Accept and tolerate those imperfections and oddities in each other." If not, these will be a source of tension in your marriage that can result in stagnation. When we are first dating, engaged, or newly married, we are in that infatuation stage and headed to the honeymoon phase; therefore, we are much more accepting of our differences. However, as the relationship moves into the dilapidation phase, repeated offenses will upset us. If that offense is not handled properly, conflict will begin, fighting can ensue, and then stagnation will occur.

Handling Offenses

It was 6:30 on a Tuesday evening, and Cheri walked in the door with a few bags of groceries. I had been wondering why she wasn't home from work yet, and now I knew why. She yelled into the living room, "Why are there soup bowls in the sink?" I replied sarcastically, "Uh, because we ate soup." This didn't make her happy, and I had no idea why. "I thought you, the boys, and I would eat together," she said. I replied in a not-so-caring tone that we don't *always* have to eat together. After all, we live together, and we see each other every day! Cheri began getting more frustrated with me and said I should have called her to discuss dinner. I guess I didn't make the situation any better by saying, "Well, it's after 6:30, you weren't home, and we were hungry!" because she stormed down the hall into the bedroom mumbling something about how she works all day and *someone* has to go grocery shopping! I didn't want the entire night to be ruined, so I just let her go and calm down. Needless to say, the rest of our evening was quiet because the situation was never resolved. As a matter of fact, the next morning, when Cheri saw that the soup bowls were still in the sink, it rekindled her anger, and she lashed out at me for not making coffee—a completely different reason that had nothing to do with soup bowl incident. Then it ruined both of our days.

The two primary ways people handle offenses is by using their fight or flight instincts. This ultimately means they will make it known that they are offended (fight) or they will ignore the offense (flight) because they don't want to create conflict. Both reactions can create difficulties in the relationship. With our soup bowl argument, Cheri was in fight mode, and I was in flight mode.

Fight Response: Overreacting

When we get offended and angry, we may become reactionary. Sometimes this reaction will hurt our spouse and make them feel the hurt that we feel. We may hurl insults at each other like weapons. By a show of force, we want our spouse, who initially hurt us, to feel even more hurt so they know not to mess with us ever again. We escalate our hurts back and forth to show our spouse that we can't be pushed around, and we leave a wake of destruction. Our soup bowl argument didn't necessarily escalate into a "wake of destruction," but it did create tension and distance between us for almost two days. In our past relationships, these arguments turned into kicking doors in, throwing physical objects, or yelling vicious words that cut so deep that after 20 years, we can still recall every detail. Those moments were indeed wakes of destruction.

In a marriage, we know our spouse's sensitive areas, those hot buttons. We know just the right weapons to use that will hit the bullseye of that button and cause a fire within them. Have you been there? In a mean spirit, have you ever called someone a name? Have you reminded someone you love of a time when they offended you as you continued to throw it in their face? That is what the devil does. He is the accuser of the brethren (Rev. 12:10). So when you find yourself reminding someone you love of a past sin, that is the devil attacking. He is constantly telling God about past sins, labeling us like the world does.

Flight Response: Ignoring the Offense

When we truly accept the idiosyncrasies of our spouse, we actually aren't offended, and there is no conflict. However, when you are truly offended, ignoring the issues creates unresolved conflict. Unresolved conflict can lead to bitterness, which is not healthy and will cause bigger problems.

When I didn't follow Cheri into the bedroom to try to understand her and resolve the argument, it made things worse. I became distant and cold toward her. I was angry at her for overreacting about something so petty.

Anger is a physical and emotional reaction when someone has wronged you. If we hang on to our anger and if we don't resolve our hurt feelings or offenses, it will turn into bitterness. Bitterness comes from unresolved anger, and it's destructive and one of the few things that destroys the container holding it—you.

Ephesians 4:31–32 is packed full of godly wisdom and is one of my favorite passages in the Bible. It is the basic guidance we all need to follow to have strong relationships:

> *Let all bitterness, and wrath, and anger, and clamour, and evil speaking, be put away from you, with all malice: ³²And be ye kind one to another, tenderhearted, forgiving one another, even as God for Christ's sake hath forgiven you.*

God's Word is telling us to "put away" bitterness, wrath, anger, clamor (yelling), and evil speaking (name calling) and to guard our hearts against bitterness taking root. if we don't guard our hearts, it will come out.

> *Luke 6:45 – A good man out of the good treasure of his heart bringeth forth that which is good; and an evil man out of the evil treasure of his heart bringeth forth that which is evil: for of the abundance of the heart his mouth speaketh.*

Luke 6:45 indicates that if we have bitter hearts, our words will reflect that inward attitude. We will express it outwardly, like Ephesians 4:31, in evil speaking, clamor, and wrath.

People will offend us, and we will get hurt; it's part of life. Offenses or hurts don't come through any fault of our own. Unfortunately, we live in a hurtful world where people are self-focused. We can choose to "fight" out the problem right away, which could be reactionary and doesn't allow our emotions to calm down, or we may choose to ignore it, which just delays the inevitable. Either way, it won't be resolved the right way, and we may become bitter. Bitter people don't forgive easily and are typically quite angry.

Let's go back to that powerful passage in Ephesians 4. We are told to avoid anger and bitterness and to learn to forgive, not for the benefit of the one that has hurt us but for our own benefit. People that are bitter are under a tremendous burden. They carry a heavy weight around with them. The problem with bitterness is that it doesn't sit stagnant in our lives; it grows and festers. It's like a container of leftover peas in the fridge. The lid is on it; moisture is forming inside the damp, dark refrigerator; and no one wants to crack open the lid for fear of seeing mold. So they put it back and let someone else deal with it later. But later turns into days, and the mold continues to grow, making it that much more offensive. Bitterness resides in our heart and comes out in other ways. Your unresolved anger turns into bitterness, which results in wrath, evil speaking, and clamor (i.e., everything that hurts other people).

Matthew 12:34 – O generation of vipers, how can ye, being evil, speak good things? for out of the abundance of the heart the mouth speaketh.

Do you know someone that is consistently negative and pessimistic? These are signs of past hurts they received that have gone unresolved, and the person that hurt them has not been forgiven, which has resulted in bitterness. The problem with bitterness is that it infects others around us. Our negativity and bitterness affect others that probably had nothing to do with the issue in the first place. Have you ever gotten mad at someone at work but took it out on your family at home? If your heart is bitter, it's hard to turn it off and hard to see the good in anything. If we don't deal with it, we will hurt the people that we love, and that hurts God. Then we will find ourselves in a place that hurts our walk with God.

Correct Response

Expressing your anger over a trespass or offense needs to be done properly to be effective. When we are offended, we want the other person to understand why we are offended. Being understood produces feelings of love and closeness. Second only to a strong relationship with God, we should strive for a strong relationship with others. God provides us joy, and next to God, the greatest source of our joy is having a strong and joy-filled relationship with the people we care about—our spouses, children, parents, siblings, friends, neighbors, and coworkers. The converse is also true. The biggest source of distress or anxiety doesn't come from financial or health difficulties but from strained or broken relationships.

Now let's go back to that soup bowl incident between Cheri and me. In hindsight, Cheri should have immediately let me know that she was hurt by my sarcastic response: "Because we ate soup." Seeing her gently say something like "Well, I guess it is late and you all were probably hungry, but it kind of hurts my feelings that you and the boys ate dinner without me and didn't even call me." This response would have immediately allowed me to better understand her, and it may have generated compassion toward her. We also would have discussed that in the future, she and I needed to call one another and discuss dinner plans. This would have made for a peaceful, happy evening, and the next day wouldn't have been ruined either.

But we didn't do things the right way. Thankfully, the Bible gives us the proper way to resolve conflict:

Luke 17:3 — Take heed to yourselves: If thy brother trespass against thee, rebuke him; and if he repent, forgive him.

Conflict resolution comes in three easy steps: rebuke, repent, and forgive. These steps are meant to help us understand one another and draw closer to one another by meeting the need for understanding.

If you recall from the introduction, the number one reason for failed marriages is "incompatibility." When we feel like the other person doesn't understand us or that we "just don't get along," that can possibly trigger us to eventually find someone else who "gets" us. We have a disagreement at home, we fight with our spouse and they are unable or unwilling to compromise, then the next thing we know, we start thinking, *They just don't understand me* or *We aren't compatible anymore*. This can be especially true if we find a sympathetic family member or friend that only hears our side of the story and emboldens us to continue to dig our heels in as they tell us how awful our spouse is being. Then we meet that co-worker or new friend that just seems to understand everything about us, and we hyper-focus on how they just aren't like our spouse. *They really get me*, and the next thing you know, an affair of the heart has begun.

While Cheri and her ex-husband were in the dilapidation phase, when they felt hopeless, Cheri began baring her soul to a friend who was just as miserable in her marriage as Cheri was. They would meet after work or talk on the phone for hours complaining about their husbands and comparing lives. This was a destructive relationship to have. Her friend was only hearing

Cheri's side of the story, and she was encouraging her to continue to see the faults in her husband and to continue to seek a life separated from him. Now, this wasn't an "affair," but it was a destructive relationship that made her hyper-focus on the negative. You see, Cheri's friend "got her," and this gave Cheri the courage to continue to choose separation instead of reparation.

Conflict is two different ways of thinking of something, and you will not see the same issue the same way. Communicating when you're offended is different than other conversations. These are what we call critical conversations. The goal is to help the other person understand our viewpoint. In any relationship, especially our marriages, we need to communicate our opinions in a way that is constructive, non-combative, and safe to lead to a successful resolution. Before we communicate, we need to prepare.

Preparing to Listen

Good communication techniques will make conflict resolution easier. Unlike other conversations, conflict resolution needs to be done with more preparation and careful consideration. I classify these as critical conversations. The whole point of the conversation is to convey our feelings and to help the other person understand us better, which draws us closer. Understanding must occur on both sides of the conversation. Most people will naturally defend their hurtful actions as unintentional, subsequently trying to be understood too.

During a critical conversation, both parties must play the role of the listener and the speaker. When two people are talking and both are giving an opinion, who is really listening? We need to be listening while the other person is talking. It's a very simple concept that we all know but few of us truly follow. If the only purpose of having a discussion is to push an opinion and be right, then listening doesn't really happen, and nothing can be resolved. We all have a need to be understood, and since love is meeting the needs of others, listening is one way we demonstrate love.

However, some people are too concerned with what they want to say and don't practice listening. When we really stop to listen and communicate well, we meet the need of understanding; in turn, that will strengthen the relationship. God created us, and he knows how hard it is for us to listen. He tells us in James 1:19 to listen:

> *Wherefore, my beloved brethren, let every man be swift to hear, slow to speak, slow to wrath:*

Don't be too hard on yourself. We all struggle with effective listening, especially in an argument. We just want the other person to hear our point of view. We sometimes sit there while they are talking but don't listen. Instead, we are rehearsing our rebuttal before the speaker can finish their point. We can't really listen if we are only focused on what *we* want to say.

I know this is cliché, but we all need to go back to what we were taught in preschool: to take turns talking. Additionally, when the other person is talking, be fully present. Really try to get inside their head and understand how they might have seen something through their point of view. That is what they are really seeking.

STEP 1: REBUKE

Before we begin to rebuke others, it is good to take time to prepare our hearts. We don't want to say anything out of anger but rather gently, with meekness, communicate how this person's actions made us feel:

> *James 1:19b–21 – "slow to wrath:* [20] *For the wrath … worketh not the righteousness of God.* [21] *Wherefore lay apart all filthiness and superfluity and receive with <u>meekness</u> the engrafted word, which is able to save your souls.*

When people are angry, they tend not to think rationally and let their emotions get the best of them. Therefore, we should take some measures to get our anger under control to help maintain our meek spirit. Meekness means to have a mild attitude that will not escalate the conflict but rather reduce the friction. Just like oil acts as a lubricant to reduce the friction of all the moving parts in an engine, meekness is a demeanor that also reduces friction. So we should be slow to get angry and not let ourselves escalate offenses.

When we are offended and get hot under the collar, we should cool down. We need to get ourselves under control and look at things objectively. One thing that normally does that for me is time away and prayer. Like verse 21 says, we can use "the engrafted word" (the Bible) to help us gain objectivity and put on a meek spirit. This passage tells us to be slow to anger, to act with meekness, and to use the engrafted word. Doing so will improve our relationships and save our marriages.

I promise you that if you properly prepare before handling conflict, you will have a more effective conversation with less strife and opposition. We need to make it safe for the other person to share their thoughts by listening and responding without losing our tempers, being reactive, or prideful, which, if you remember, is leading in the flesh. This will only escalate the hurt feelings, and then you will have two people that are offended, making it more difficult to resolve. Creating a safe environment to talk will make the other person feel more open to share their own feelings and better able to understand us.

Webster's dictionary defines rebuke as "to reprehend for a fault."[12] Rebuke isn't getting the other person to shoulder all the blame nor is it to make yourself look better than them. The Bible's goal of rebuke is to reach a reconciliation and reunification. We all have responsibility in any conflict; we just need to realize this truth before we start to reconcile or have the critical conversation.

Most people, especially our spouses and closest friends, don't want to purposely hurt our feelings. When we get angry and seek to hurt another out of revenge, that is wrath. When we think more of ourselves and less of other people, that is pride. Let's come to the table with the goal of helping them understand the offense

---

12 http://webstersdictionary1828.com/Dictionary/rebuke

while being open to what part we may have had in any miscommunication, and with a meek demeanor, we will resolve that conflict in no time.

Those that love us don't want to purposely upset us. I know I just said this, but it's worth repeating because we *all* struggle to realize this. Understanding that they didn't intend to hurt us is to assume noble intent. If we realize they didn't purposely want to hurt us, we can then begin to understand their way of thinking, which helps to resolve the conflict:

> *Proverbs 25:8 – Go not forth hastily to strive, lest thou know not what to do in the end thereof, when thy neighbour hath put thee to shame.*

Proverbs 25:8 is basically telling us not to jump to conclusions and react with strife or anger. We should always do our research, ask questions, and don't assume. We'll find that once we search out the matter and realize the facts, we will probably end up embarrassed at our reaction. We need to assume that the other person loves us, has our best interests at heart, and isn't out to hurt us.

It was a hectic Monday morning, and as I thought about everything I needed to do that day, I began to stress. My wife, moved with compassion, offered to pick up my dry cleaning for me. Knowing I had an important meeting the next morning, I wanted to make sure I had a specific suit that was at the cleaners, so I politely declined. She insisted. Thankful for the help, I allowed her to do this one thing for me. With her doing that, it allowed me to focus on other things I needed to do and still get home at a reasonable hour later that night. When I walked in the door around 8 p.m., we kissed, we talked about our day, and I asked her if she had gone to the dry cleaners. She had a look of shock when she realized she didn't do what she not only offered to do but insisted she would do. To top it off, the dry cleaners closed at 7:00, and I needed to leave the house before they opened the next morning.

How would you react? Stop and think about it for a minute.

I can tell you my initial reaction was not good. I was angry! After a long day and being exhausted, I barked out, "That is why I wanted to get the dry cleaning myself! I guess I really can't rely on anyone for anything." Then I walked into the bedroom and slammed the door. What a blow to her. She already felt bad, and I had just made her feel worse. But this is what the devil wants. He wants us to think no one can meet our needs but us, that no one can love us except ourselves. The devil wants us to think the worst about the other person.

While in the bedroom, once I calmed down, I began to pray. God started to soften my heart and made me realize that my wife didn't want to hurt me and must have a good reason and that I was wrong for my hurtful words and actions. After I cooled down and thought about what I had done, I returned to the kitchen and told her how sorry I was for yelling. I also told her that I knew she wouldn't deliberately disappoint me and that I was sure there was a good reason for not picking up the dry cleaning. She explained that she had had a long day too and that she had intended to get the dry cleaning. She was truly sorry, and she was overwhelmed by things that had happened at work. She was so focused on just getting home that stopping at the dry cleaners completely slipped her mind.

If I had allowed my wife to explain why she didn't pick up the dry cleaning, we may not have had that argument. I know that I would not have hurt my wife with my words and actions, and we would not have had the stress. Isn't that what the devil wants? He wants us to be offended, and he wants us to have stressful relationships, especially in our marriages. He doesn't want people to be close to one another.

We need to assume noble intent by the other person. The best way to do that is to continue to focus each and every day on all the positive things our spouses do for us. In a word, *gratitude*. Each night when I pray, I recall all the things that others have done for me that day and how God worked through others to be a blessing for me. It's impossible to have both negative *and* positive thoughts about someone at the same time:

James 3:11 – Doth a fountain send forth at the same place sweet water and bitter?

Our minds can only focus on one or the other. If we continue to train our minds to focus on the positive things, then it gets easier to assume noble intent. However, if we start listening to the devil and think negative things about others, it will harden our hearts and make us bitterer.

Like everything in life, timing is everything. Make sure the timing is right to have that difficult conversation. We want an environment without distractions. Aside from ensuring we have more time to talk, we should be rested and fed. There have been times when Cheri and I have gotten into an argument before work. There is no time to resolve it the right way, and that probably leads to more issues. The focus of the listener will more than likely be on what their next comment is, and they won't necessarily be focused on resolving the argument. Additionally, there shouldn't be other distractions either. If the TV or computer is on, turn them off. Put your phone away or turn it off. If it is not a good time to discuss and if you can't have their full, undivided attention, then it's better to agree to talk at a later time.

I will say that it's better to be late to work or a social commitment to resolve a conflict than to let it fester and move on about your day. Reconciliation is an ongoing process and should take priority over most commitments; otherwise, your hurt feelings may creep into other conversations and actions, causing more hurt feelings with our spouse and others.

After we ensure we have the proper amount of time and the proper environment without distraction, it's time to get to the root of the problem. Typically, we get offended because of one of four things:

1. Something someone said
2. Something someone did

3. Something someone didn't say

4. Something someone didn't do

One or more of these four actions will make us offended. Our opening to the critical conversation must be specific and concise and will take the form of "when you...I feel...." For example, when I say, "**When you** *yell at me in front of the kids,* **I feel** *embarrassed,*" the listener can quickly understand what I said and how it made me feel.

In this scenario, the burden of communicating effectively is on me; therefore, being specific and concise helps me quickly get to the action that caused the offense and work through the problem without causing more confusion.

Proverbs 10:19 – "In the multitude of words there wanteth not sin: but he that refraineth his lips is wise."

Let's assume that I said, "**When you** *are mean,* **I feel** *hurt.*" The listener's brain starts to immediately process: "Mean? How was I mean? What did I say or do?" Every word after "mean" is lost on the listener. However, in our first example, we helped their brain laser focus on the specific issue, which will allow for the conversation to be more effective and get resolved more quickly.

Also, the second example, "when you are mean...," may be perceived by the listener as a bit confrontational, and we begin to stack another offense on top of the original. Now the listener is offended as well, and we start to compound the problem rather than solve it. Carefully choosing our words is critical to this conversation. Sometimes our natural reaction to being offended is to lash back with "I'm mean? Well, you are a ___!" Proverbs 12:18 tells us that our words can hurt just like being stabbed with a sword and can be wielded like weapons.

There is that speaketh like the piercings of a sword: but the tongue of the wise is health.

During these critical conversations, we need to carefully consider our words because whether intentional or not, provocative words can result in causing distance rather than reconciliation. We need to specifically shape our message so that it doesn't sound like we are blaming the listener, or they will naturally be resistant to the message you are trying to communicate.

We live in a society of people with short attention spans, although long-winded conversations are great when you both agree. In fact, many times my wife will finish my sentences for me because, as you all know now, I'm typically long winded. But if you really want the listener to hear you and if you really want them to pay attention, you need to get your point across quickly. By being concise and non-confrontational, you are helping to communicate more effectively and are well on your way to reconciliation.

STEP 2: REPENT

This step is for the one that performed the hurtful action. The goal of repentance is to show remorse (We know you didn't mean to hurt them.) and to better understand your own behavior (words or actions) and how you made the other person feel. Hopefully, through your awareness, you will do things differently in the future.

Remorse

Once you clearly understand how you offended someone, it's time to respond. The key in our response is to communicate to our spouse that we care and to clarify that our offense was not on purpose. Once they know we didn't intend to hurt them, it will defuse the conflict and bring us closer together.

Something such as "I'm sorry I (insert what you said, did, didn't say, or didn't do). Will you forgive me?" will show remorse for hurt feelings. Simply saying, "I'm sorry," is insufficient because you aren't stating what you are apologizing for. Your apology must communicate clearly and concisely what you did to hurt their feelings for the healing process to begin. As the offender, ask clarifying questions if you aren't sure you understand exactly how you offended them. It's perfectly fine to ask if there was anything else you did.

People sometimes go astray when they are trying to resolve issues by excusing their behavior: "Well, if you didn't do this, I wouldn't have…"; this is our pride not wanting to admit we were wrong. When we excuse the behavior and when we turn the tables to become the victim, this will convey to our spouses (the offended) that we didn't understand or care about their hurt. This will not resolve the issue but will only make it worse. If we really love them and care for them, we will try to understand their hurt and apologize for any offense, regardless of whether or not it was intentional.

Future Behavior

Repentance is a fancy way in the Bible to say, "I will think differently about this action." Spouses don't intentionally offend each other. (Yes, I said it again because we struggle to realize this.) As the offender, understanding what we did and how that hurt someone can help us change our future behavior to avoid those offensive actions. The future actions may be hard to do but should be based upon really understanding how you hurt them and offering not to do it again.

Now that we realize we've hurt someone's feelings and we have apologized for the offense, we should shift to solving the problem by avoiding future arguments. Remember, in a strong relationship, we don't purposely go out of our way to hurt the other person.

Learning and understanding our spouses' boundaries help us not to trespass against them (cross those boundaries) and thus offend them again. Once the offended person knows that we understand what we did to offend them, we need to convey that we will act less offensive in the future by saying something like

"In the future, I will...." This shows we really care about them, that we value the relationship, and that we don't wish to upset them. Don't offer to do something you aren't willing to do, and make sure you pray about it to let God help you avoid a similar incident.

A lot of times we don't realize what we did offended someone, and the awareness of this is a big step. If we are more aware of our offending behavior, we can be better equipped not to repeat it.

Job 6:24 – Teach me, and I will hold my tongue: and cause me to understand wherein I have erred.

When we are patient and consoling and when we are meek with one another, we become of one mind and one mouth, and we glorify God. Our acceptance gives people comfort, and they will feel closer to us.

Psalm 133:1– Behold, how good and how pleasant it is for brethren to dwell together in unity!

God wants us to be in harmony with one another as we are all God's children. We need to let his Holy Spirit change people and let our hearts simply show love and accept them for how God made them.

STEP 3: FORGIVENESS
Now that all the issues are on the table and both parties completely understand one another, it's time for the final step: forgiveness.

THE NEED FOR FORGIVENESS

Once the apology has been communicated, the person who was offended must forgive. Every strong relationship must have forgiveness.

Psalm 86:5 – For thou, Lord, art good, and ready to forgive; and plenteous in mercy unto all them that call upon thee.

God knows that bitterness and not forgiving are fatal to a relationship. Don't allow insecurity and fear to prevent you from forgiving. Perhaps your defenses kick in to guard your heart from future pain. You think, *They'll probably hurt me again, and I'll feel this pain all over again* or *I can choose to forgive and then they'll hurt me again; then I'll look foolish.*

It's normal to have our defenses up after we have been hurt. However, if someone truly has repented (changed their mind) and has shown remorse, they are not likely to repeat behavior that purposely hurts people they love. When you were a newly saved Christian, you most likely reflected on your prior life of sin and looked at it differently. Once you understood that you had hurt God, yourself, and other people through your actions, you changed your attitude toward that sin (repentance) and felt bad about all your previously destructive actions (remorse). In fact, you probably were determined not to repeat that sinful behavior after you were saved.

> Romans 6:1–2 – *¹What shall we say then? Shall we continue in sin, that grace may abound? ²God forbid. How shall we, that are dead to sin, live any longer therein?*

I have been on the receiving end of bitterness and unforgiveness. My ex is still angry for things I did to her while we were together even though I have apologized and asked for her forgiveness. Throughout our son's life, we would interact at soccer games, school concerts, parent–teacher conferences, prom, and high school graduation. While I feel I have done all I can to seek forgiveness and I don't harbor any ill will toward her, she, on the other hand, goes out of her way to avoid me and looks absolutely miserable when she has to be in the same room with me. I'm emotionally free, but she has put herself in a prison of negativity. When you choose not to forgive, you think you are holding the other person hostage, but in actuality, you are the one imprisoning yourself.

Forgiveness happens when you decide to stop holding the offense over the head of the other person after they have apologized and after they have shown remorse. Don't be afraid to forgive. Start to free yourself from that bondage by forgiving. If you don't forgive, it will destroy your relationships. Forgiveness is the most powerful thing you can do and the one thing you have complete control over.

When it comes to forgiving your spouse, if you realize no one is perfect (including you), it becomes easier to forgive. At the foot of the cross, we all fall short (Romans 3:23). Their struggles might be different than yours, but we all have them. When I am alone with God and praying to him to forgive my sins, it starts to make me feel hypocritical if I don't want to forgive my spouse of hers. When we focus on our own sins and not on their sins, we will be kind to one another, tenderhearted, and forgiving one another, not for their sake but for Christ's sake (Eph. 4:32).

If the steps within REPENT – REBUKE – FORGIVE are followed properly, we will feel reconnected, and the healing will begin. We need to accept our spouses' idiosyncrasies, understand their boundaries, and be patient with their shortcomings by gently rebuking when they offend us.

Our actions should be spiritually led, and we should be focused on being "doers of the word, and not hearers only" (James 1:22). We are never done growing as Christians. We all have things to work on, and someday, when we pass from this life, our construction will be done and our sin nature will be gone. Until then, we need to continue to learn, continue to grow, and live peaceably among all men.

Victory Over Past Bitterness

New relationships don't typically have deep-rooted bitterness. However, your past relationships can bring bitterness into current relationships. Fixing our bitter hearts due to past hurts helps our current relationships to be stronger and more unified.

When an offense happens, we have to deal with our anger, hurt, and disappointment immediately. We can't let it germinate in our hearts but must prevent the bitter heart proactively by dealing with issues when they happen.

Are you thinking to yourself as you read this, *"But you don't know what they did…you don't know what a monster that person is…?* I may not know what that person did to you, but I do know God expects you to forgive, and if we don't forgive others, God won't forgive us:

> *Matthew 6:12, 15 – And forgive us our debts, as we forgive our debtors…. But if ye forgive not men their trespasses, neither will your Father forgive your trespasses.*

If we harbor bitterness, then we should expect God to harbor bitterness against us:

> *Matthew 18:21–22 – [21]Then came Peter to him, and said, Lord, how oft shall my brother sin against me, and I forgive him? till seven times? [22]Jesus saith unto him, I say not unto thee, Until seven times: but, Until seventy times seven.*

Peter asked Jesus, "How often should I forgive? Seven times?" Jesus said, "Don't forgive seven times but 70 times seven times." When I do the math, that is 490 times. No one I know will take the time to keep a log and track something like this over the course of their life. Basically, Jesus told Peter to forgive them every time. Imagine if a good friend of mine borrowed my car and got a scratch on my paint. Then he profusely apologizes and says, "I promise I won't do it again." Then he asks to borrow my car again and he returns it with a dent in the bumper. At this point, I might start getting angry. But let's say I let him borrow my car a third time, and BANG, he damages it again! What if he continued damaging my car seven times in a row and I still forgave him? Wouldn't that be unusual? Almost impossible? But then Christ makes it exponential: seven times 70, too numerous to count!

God won't command us to do something he wouldn't do himself. God forgave *you* for Christ's sake. Why does He forgive? Because of what Christ did on the cross. Christ took the punishment for all of our sins so that we can be forgiven not just seven times but *every* time. If we focus on the crime, on the hurt, we will hate and resent the person that is the focus of our anger. That is why we don't forgive them for *their* sake but for Christ's sake. Think about how God forgave you. If you focus on your own offenses, on your own sins, you realize how imperfect you are and how amazing God's grace and mercy are, and it will become a whole lot easier to forgive. But if we focus on their offenses, we will not forgive.

Forgiving Is Not Forgetting

Forgiving doesn't require forgetting. When I was a young child, I was running through the house chasing my brother. When he ran out the back door, he slammed the door made of glass as I turned the corner. Instinctively, I put my hand out to stop the door, and my hand went through it. The glass painfully tore through my wrist, blood running down my arm. As a three-year-old, this event was very traumatic, and as you can tell, I still vividly remember the details of the event. However, I no longer feel the pain of that glass tearing my skin. I have not forgotten the event, but it no longer hurts. That is forgiveness. Forgiveness is letting go of the pain that memory causes us. The scar remains on my wrist today, but I sometimes forget what hand it's on because the pain is gone. When we start to forgive, we slowly start to remove the pain of the event until we only have the memory, not the pain.

Many struggle with the worldly phrase of "forgive and forget" since they are two separate actions. Forgiveness is not forgetting; it's just refusing to use the past against someone. Just like in a court of law, the facts become inadmissible, and we decide we will not stack up offenses. Isn't that how God forgives? When you confess your sins, they are gone. They are washed in the blood of Jesus Christ. They aren't hidden behind God's back but are as far as the east is from the west (Ps. 103:12). In God's eyes, once we ask for forgiveness, it's as if it never happened. But even though we forgive, unfortunately, we can't always forget.

Forgiveness is not using it against someone, and it's not bringing it up over and over. Forgiveness is letting go of the anger. There may be some people in your life who have hurt you and whom you no longer associate with. Perhaps this is because your life took you away from them or you chose to not continue to have a relationship with them. Regardless, the choice to forgive still must happen.

Forgiveness is not seeking revenge. God will punish that person.

> Romans 12:19 – Dearly beloved, avenge not yourselves, but rather give place unto wrath: for it is written, Vengeance is mine; I will repay, saith the Lord.

Forgiveness is choosing to forgive them by asking God to help you forgive and then moving on, whether physically or emotionally.

Cheri's Testimony on Forgiving

It's been just over 17 years since my ex-husband and I separated. As I sit here and recall the exact moment when I packed a bag and left, all the memories and the feelings I had are crystal clear. I was scared, upset, overwhelmed, confused, exhausted, and hopeless. I can sit here with confidence and describe how I was feeling, but I can no longer feel the pain of the event.

To get to the point of forgiveness, you need to understand how my ex-husband and I got to the point of separation. The foundation of our problem started with me. At that point in my life, I did not have a personal relationship with God. I believed in God and knew all the stories of Jesus and his disciples, but I didn't pray and didn't read the Bible. (I didn't even own a Bible!) I had a relationship with Cheri and Cheri only. It was all about me. I looked at everything in life from the perspective of "How will this affect me?"

My ex-husband didn't have a relationship with God either. He wasn't even sure he truly believed in God. You see, his sister died suddenly when she was only 14, his parents divorced, and a few years later, his older brother died at age 28. He was angry at God and questioned how there could be a God if he let such bad things happen. My ex never really dealt with this anger, so at times, it came out in his actions.

I wasn't happy unless my circumstances were happy. If my ex-husband and I were spending time together and having fun, then I was happy. If we had friends over and our kids were all playing together, I was happy. If I got down to a smaller size, I was happy. It was always "IF."

From the beginning of our relationship, we had financial struggles. We never lived within our means. We would go out to dinner and charge it. We would go on vacation and charge it. We would upgrade our car and get a bigger loan. The banks loved us. I knew that living outside of our means was not healthy for our relationship or our future, but buying stuff made me happy too.

When I was about 27 (about the time we married), I was diagnosed with endometriosis, which caused infertility. I didn't have extreme stages of it, but the doctor told me that we would need infertility treatment if we ever wanted our own child. By the grace of God, I got pregnant on my own, without infertility treatment. Oh, how I loved being a new mom! A.J. was my world, and I truly didn't know selfless love until I held him in my arms. For the first time, I put someone else's needs before my own.

When A.J. was around two, I wanted another baby, and we agreed that we would start trying. Well, the endometriosis had gotten worse, and this time it wasn't happening without science helping out. So I threw myself into researching infertility and all the available methods of conception. On my night stand sat an ovulation thermometer and a chart where I'd take my temperature every morning and document the results. After three months of tracking, it was evident that I was not ovulating and therefore I could not get pregnant on my own. Without going into the details, we followed an infertility method where the doctor told us what days we should have sex. Being intimate with each other became a science project. It was loveless and deliberate. After months of this, I was finally pregnant, but within four weeks, I miscarried. It was probably the most devastating loss I had experienced in my life thus far. I had fallen in love with a child I would never get to hold. I had fallen in love with the idea of another baby to love me back, but that would never happen. I had fallen into a depression that I couldn't get out of, and the depression then led to bitterness. I would see a pregnant woman, and daggers would shoot from my eyes to hers. My ex-husband didn't understand. What made it worse was that he didn't seem to be upset like I was, and that made me bitter toward him too. I shut down and didn't open up to him about how I felt. He wasn't sharing how he felt either. It was conflict avoidance at its best.

I can honestly say that this was the breaking point of our marriage. I threw myself into A.J. and his three-and-a-half-year-old life. Everything I did was for him—not my ex-husband and not even for me. I emotionally left our marriage long before I physically left.

About a year before we actually split up, I decided that I should try harder to make it work. I bought two copies of Dr. Phil's book, *Relationship Rescue*, one for me and one for him, and gave it to him for Valentine's Day. I read the first couple chapters and never picked it up again. He admitted he never read any of it. We had appointments to see a marriage counselor, but we never went. Neither one of us was trying anymore, so I told him we needed a break to decide if the marriage was worth saving and that I was taking our son to my parents' house for a few weeks. He was overcome with anger. This argument turned physical, and by the next day, I had packed a bag for A.J. and me, and we left.

Sometime around 2008, after I turned to God for help, after I realized I couldn't do life without him, and after I admitted I was a sinner, I began to think back on all these things. Up until this point, I was always blaming my ex and others, and I now realized that my sinful, selfish ways contributed to the breakup of our marriage and the destruction of our family. It was at this moment that I no longer felt anger toward my ex-husband. I didn't have a taste of bitterness in my mouth when I spoke his name. I didn't feel vengeance toward him. That was not Cheri; that was all God!

My ex was meeting me after church one Sunday to pick up A.J. Right there in our church parking lot, on the same property where I had learned so much about God and how a godly wife and mother is supposed to act, I apologized to my son's father. With A.J. standing by my side, I looked into my ex-husband's eyes and said, "I want you to know that I have forgiven you for the things you did during our marriage. I would like to apologize for the role I played in our marriage ending because I know I did a lot wrong too. I am truly sorry. Will you forgive me?"

He was taken by complete surprise over what I had just said. It's still a little fuzzy as to what his response was, but that doesn't really matter. I forgave him. I apologized to him. I asked him to forgive me. Whether he chooses to forgive me or not doesn't matter. I have no control over his heart. I only have control over mine.

I kissed my son goodbye and walked to the car, where Eric was standing, watching from a distance. I had never felt so free!

5

FOUNDATIONAL NEEDS

Foundational needs are an essential part of our happiness. These needs are so critical that if ALL other needs are met yet just one of the foundational needs is not met, we will not be happy. Those foundational needs are below:

- Energy renewal
- Safety
- Shelter
- Sustenance
- Financial stability

Imagine that you have a job you love and lots of quality friendships, but the home you live in never has hot water, crime is happening right next to you, and the AC and heat never work; you would not be very satisfied. Most of these foundational needs are physical, and having our physical needs met is something we take for granted. In other words, *just* having our physical needs met won't make us happy, but without them, we can become very unhappy.

I've included financial stability because it is the primary means by which we can supply the other needs in our life. Having a steady income ensures we can pay for these essential physical needs.

ENERGY RENEWAL

How long can you work before you need a break? The typical work day is eight hours plus unpaid periodic breaks; add on your commute time, and that makes a typical day at least nine hours. The recommended daily amount of sleep for most adults is seven hours a day. That leaves about eight hours of your day to eat, shower, exercise, do house/yard work, read the Bible, pray, take care of family, etc. Before you know it, you have very little time for yourself. But isn't that what God wants in a selfless Christian?

It is true that God wants us to think of others more than we think of ourselves, but no one can continue to be on the go every waking hour. Eventually we will burn out. When we burn out, we are no good to anyone, including God. The Bible teaches us that we need to be hard workers and that we should not be lazy.

Proverbs 6:6 – Go to the ant, thou sluggard; consider her ways, and be wise:

We also need time to recreate. Didn't God rest on the seventh day after working six days to create the universe and the earth (Gen. 2:2)? God rested after working hard, and he wants us to rest as well. We need to re-create ourselves. Recreation is expected after we have worked hard. There is a rule in my house that we have "fun time" after our work is done. When our boys were younger, they were not allowed to turn on TV, play video games, or go outside with friends until their homework and chores were done.

Recent studies show that we perform optimally in 90-minute sprints followed by a 10-minute break. These work periods are highly focused on a single task, where the employees are fully focused. Employees that adopted this pattern got more work done in an eight-hour day than others that took shorter breaks, used their breaks to check on work email, or pushed the 90-minute sprint to 120 minutes. Without a proper break time, we end up pushing ourselves by using caffeine, eating sugary snacks, or simply using our own adrenaline, which causes us to crash at the tail end of our work day—when we get home. Is it fair to our family to come home after a long day unable to spend time with them the way we need us to? We end up giving the ones we love the most our "leftovers." We also may not pull our fair share of the work around the house, or we could be irritable and take it out on our family because we are tired. This is not fair to our spouse and our kids.

The bottom line is that we all need a break to maximize our efficiency and keep us working at our peak performance. The question is, how do we recreate in a way that helps us perform well in our next task? The answer is "It depends."

I married an extrovert. Cheri loves to be around other people. When she is in a crowded room with lots of people doing lots of things, she is energized. So her ideal break time is spent chatting with friends and co-workers, calling her parents, calling me, and just connecting with other people in a positive way. Most of her family is the same way. We often attend or host parties with her immediate family. My wife is most energized when our three boys, her parents, her three sisters, their husbands, and the seven nieces and nephews and their spouses and children are all at our house. That is now more than 25 people at family gatherings, and my wife absolutely loves the energy and excitement. She likes to connect to those family members, catch up on what they are doing, discuss current events, and enjoy their company.

On the other hand, I am an introvert. Those same parties are enjoyable to me because I love her family too; however, those events drain me of all my energy. Typically, the parties will last three to four hours, sometimes longer, and throughout the event, I will disappear from time to time to "recharge." The high-energy atmosphere and noise level will physically make me tired.

Meanwhile, my wife is so excited that she is ready to run a marathon after the event is over, and I just want to go in our bedroom and spend time alone in front of the TV and then fall asleep. I personally will get my energy renewal by spending time alone playing video games, doing a sudoku puzzle, or reading. My wife finds those things mildly entertaining for a brief period of time but soon will get antsy and bored.

Although we are different, we respect this about one another. We do things that may drain us of our energy in order to make sure our spouse gets that need satisfied. The key to a successful relationship is to understand how your spouse gets their energy then respect it and support it. When my wife tells me we have another party to go to, it may not be my favorite thing to do, but I know she will be renewed by it; therefore, to demonstrate my love for her, I will gladly attend. What she and I have learned over the years is to agree ahead of time how long we will stay at the event. Conversely, my wife will give me time to play video games or read because she loves me and understands that is how I renew my energy level.

SAFETY, SHELTER, AND SUSTENANCE

We all have a foundational need to feel safe, have a home (e.g., shelter), and have food (e.g., sustenance). Like other needs in this category, we typically may take these for granted. When the foundational needs of safety, shelter, or sustenance are missing, we feel threatened. This is very stressful and makes it hard to focus on anything else.

Men are called to be the primary leader, protector, and provider of the home. In Genesis 3, when Adam disobeyed God, God told Adam that because of his disobedience, he would have to work or till the ground in order to feed his family:

> [17] *And unto Adam he said, Because thou hast hearkened unto the voice of thy wife, and hast eaten of the tree, of which I commanded*

thee, saying, Thou shalt not eat of it: cursed is the ground for thy sake; in sorrow shalt thou eat of it all the days of thy life; [18]Thorns also and thistles shall it bring forth to thee; and thou shalt eat the herb of the field; [19]In the sweat of thy face shalt thou eat bread, till thou return unto the ground; for out of it wast thou taken: for dust thou art, and unto dust shalt thou return.

We see in this passage that God "cursed" the ground. He caused weeds (thorns and thistles) to grow among our crops and made us work hard just to provide for our families. God also declared Adam should rule over his wife (Gen. 3:16). So this passage tells us that the husband is responsible for his wife and is called to be the leader and provider for the home.

The Bible says husbands ought to give everything for their homes and for their wives, to provide for their needs out of love. The Bible is clear that the husband is to lead, protect, and provide for his home, including the foundational needs of safety, shelter, and sustenance.

In 19th century America, women began working outside the home in larger numbers but still didn't make as much as men and therefore couldn't support themselves financially. Finally in 1963, the United States passed the Equal Pay Act requiring equal wages for men and women. In Genesis 29, Jacob had to work 7 years for Laban in order to get permission to marry his daughter Rachel. In those days a woman would be cared for by her father until such time as she was married, and then the responsibility to care for the woman would transfer to her new husband. This is why we have the tradition of a husband asking the father for his daughter's hand in marriage and why, during the wedding ceremony, the father would walk the bride down the aisle and proclaim that he was giving his daughter away. If a father wasn't confident the young man would be able to provide for his daughter's basic needs, he would refuse to allow them to marry. This is also why people had many wives in biblical times; a marriage wasn't always sexual, but it sometimes was necessary to "take care of" another woman that was unable to provide for herself. Women weren't allowed to own property, so if their husband were to die, they would not be given the land. The land ownership (i.e., birthright) would pass on to the husband's brother. If there was no brother, the widow would be required to marry another family member (a cousin perhaps) so that she would be taken care of properly and so the land was not lost to other families.

It wasn't until more recently in our history that women were afforded more equal rights. In 1839 Mississippi became the first state to offer women the ability to own property in their own name[13]. Today women are afforded equal rights, and although we endeavor to keep some traditions of ages past, they are less necessary today. However, God did clearly create men and women differently, and that has never changed. God predisposed us to perform certain tasks within the family structure, and when we veer out of alignment, it can cause stress in our marriages and relationships. A woman can certainly be the breadwinner, and a man can stay home and raise kids, but they genetically are not as well equipped. It's like an offensive lineman and a quarterback switching positions. The quarterback will not block as effectively as a 300-pound lineman, and the linemen will probably not throw the football as far or as accurately as the quarterback. They both can play those positions, and they both have some innate skill to act in that role, but when those two people occupy their intended position, they play the game much more effectively. When husbands act as the leader and provider for the family, our families tend to operate more effectively as well.

---

13 Boswell, Angela (2000). "Married Women's Property Rights and the Challenge to the Patriarchal Order: Colorado County, Texas". In Coryell, Janet L. Negotiating Boundaries of Southern Womanhood: Dealing With the Powers That Be. University of Missouri Press. p. 92.

FINANCIAL STABILITY

In Genesis 3:23, God punished Adam by making men "till the ground." Most of us do not "till the ground" anymore, so we provide the basic needs of food and shelter by earning money outside the home. Financial issues are a leading cause of divorce because when the basic financial need is threatened, the wife or husband will start to feel unsafe. When we feel our finances are less secure, we begin to lose trust in our spouse. This could be the beginning of our spouse looking elsewhere for those needs to be met. It only takes one party in a marriage, through overspending, living beyond their means, or accumulating massive debt, to disrupt the harmony of everyone in the home. These actions make the other person feel like one of their basic needs is threatened.

How to Stabilize Your Finances

A budget is a basic plan used to allocate your money and direct your money where to go. Without a budget, people will end up running out of money because they don't track where their money went. If you don't create and follow a budget, you will lack available finances for emergency purposes.

When I was in my early twenties, I took out a car loan based on my monthly available income. I also minimized my insurance payment, so I had really high deductibles so I could afford the insurance for my new car. I was living paycheck to paycheck on my monthly salary, paying my bills on time, and spending the rest discriminately.

This was working great until one morning it was raining, I was running late, and I hit another car from behind. It was completely my fault, and now I had a $1,000 deductible to pay. I needed a car, but my next paycheck was a few weeks away. What now? I had some money in savings but not enough. I had used my discretionary funds for the month, so I had nothing left. Not only did I stress about getting my car fixed, dealing with insurance, and relying on friends to get around without a car but now I had to borrow money to pay for this emergency expense.

I ended up using a credit card, and it took me years to recover. If I had spent a few months saving for this emergency, I would be better off financially today. By mismanaging my money, I compounded my situation by adding additional unnecessary stress to an already stressful situation. If I had been married at the time, I'm sure this would have become a huge fight about our finances, and a lack of trust would have built up between my wife and me. Thank goodness I learned this lesson before my current marriage to Cheri. By establishing a budget and staying on budget you ensure you can meet the foundational needs in your marriage.

Living within Your Means

Before I get into specifics of budgeting, I want to provide a few thoughts on how to adjust to living within your means. The example above describes when I was living *at* my means. Most people live *beyond* their means, but the goal is to live *within* your means. In other words, spend less than you make. Here are a few things to keep in mind to help you do just that:

Examine your lifestyle: It doesn't matter if you have a lot of money or just a little bit of money; if you don't live within your means, you will end up with the same problem. People have a tendency to try to keep up with the Joneses. When I first graduated from college, I remember thinking that if I only had 10% more in my paycheck, I would be able to make ends meet and be happy. Year after year, I got raises but kept increasing my lifestyle. I went from basic cable to adding premium channels then adding HBO. Five years later, I had almost doubled my paycheck, and I was in the same mindset: "If I only had 10% more…"

You see, it's not how much we make but how much we spend in light of what we make. Using financial counselors, we can get an objective look at our lifestyles, and they can help us avoid any pitfalls we currently are making.

Enjoy God's resources: We live in an entertainment-saturated culture. It's difficult to imagine having fun without spending money. However, God has provided many free resources that are just as good if not better than man-made entertainment. God gave us many natural wonders that we can take in and enjoy. Next time you are strapped for cash and want to do something, pack a picnic basket, play kickball at your local park, or take a hike or walk with your spouse. Instead of plastic bottled water, fill a container at home to bring with you. Pack a lunch to avoid eating out. There is plenty to do without spending a lot of money. If we plan ahead, we can stretch our dollars further.

Establishing a Budget

There are many books written on how to budget and many software programs you can use to track your spending. I will cover some basics of budgeting in this book, but it will not cover every possible contingency nor will it be able to replace a financial advisor.

Step 1: Identify your earnings.
The income we earn MUST determine our spending. For most people, the only source of income is their wages. However, there may be other sources of income, including investment income, government support, trust funds, etc. Guidelines in a budget will be based on percentages of income, so it's important to make sure people understand all of their income before they start deciding where their income will be allocated.

Step 2: Identify your mandatory spending.

The first step in establishing a budget is to set aside money for mandatory expenses. These expenses take the form of shelter (mortgage or rent), food, clothing, medical and dental expenses, tithe, utilities, and transportation (bus fare, taxi, or automobile expense). Some financial advisors and budget software will consider transportation as discretionary spending; however, most people cannot walk to where they work and must rely on private of public transportation. For this reason, I'm going to put this into a mandatory expense; however, it is quite possible to live without owning an automobile.

Next, allocate a percentage of your income to include all mandatory expenses. Suggested allocations are as follows:

- Tithe   10%
- Housing (Rent/Mortgage)   30%
- Utilities (Electric, Oil & Gas)   5–10%
- Groceries   5–15%
- Car   5–10%
- Medical Expenses (e.g., co-pay or Rx)   2%
- Auto Maintenance & Repairs   3%
- Medical Insurance   5%
- Auto Insurance   5%
- Home Insurance   1%

These mandatory expenses tie directly into foundational needs of safety (medical), shelter (home/heat), and sustenance (food).

Step 3: Determine your savings goals.

You should endeavor to save nearly 10% each month. Your savings should be equal to six months of your monthly mandatory bills. If you lost your job for some unforeseen reason, you would be able to look for a job without the stress of losing your house, your car, or your ability to feed your family. Your savings can also be for medical, auto, or home deductibles in case disaster strikes and you need to pay that high deductible. This savings is called liquid savings because it is easily available and not tied up like an investment or retirement.

If you are thinking, *Wow, this is hard*, you are not alone. It takes time and work to build that financial foundation, but it's worth it. The Bible tells us:

> *Proverbs 13:11 – Wealth gotten by vanity shall be diminished: but he that gathereth by labour shall increase.*

If you are able to save 10–30% and get to that six-month savings goal, then you can start to invest money. We all want to retire someday, and the amount we need to save for retirement depends on our living expenses. I recommend that once you have reached your liquid savings goal, you consult a financial planner on your retirement goals and invest appropriately. Just as a rule of thumb, I would recommend you allocate at least 10% of your paycheck to a 401k, IRA, or some other retirement account. Compounded interest is a powerful thing, so it's never too early to get started.

Step 4: Identify your discretionary spending.

After mandatory bills are paid, savings are set aside, and there is some left over, then a focus can be placed on discretionary spending. Discretionary spending is spending on luxury items: things you could stop paying for at a moment's notice. Losing a luxury item may be a discomfort, but it won't threaten your job or living conditions. For example, if I lose my cable television, it's a little stressful, but I know there are some that don't pay a cable bill and don't even watch TV at all. They can get to work, can eat, and have a warm place to lay their head at night, so they are still able to function. If you can't afford to pay for groceries, that is much different than not being able to afford television. Taking my example of the earlier car accident, I struggled through my college years because of that accident. In fact, if I hadn't had free college tuition (thanks to being a veteran and the G.I. Bill), I would more than likely never have been able to go to college. But I can tell you that

I didn't have cable television. I spent time at my friend's house watching TV most nights. I didn't have Internet nor did I eat very healthy for almost four years. I was barely able to afford groceries, heat, shelter, and transportation. I took a second job, and my grades suffered because of it too. I did all of this while trying to make child support payments and spend time with my infant son. My life was not very peaceful.

Here are a few examples of discretionary spending:

- Entertainment (movies, sporting events, etc.)
- Dining out
- Discretionary utilities
  - Cable
  - Mobile phone
  - Internet
- Clothing/dry cleaning
- Other miscellaneous expenses
  - Gym membership
  - Gifts
  - Vacation
  - Pets

You may be wondering where you can get the money to go out to eat with your friends, join a gym, or afford a pet. This is where we often overspend our budget, struggle to make ends meet, and are always living off our credit cards. It starts when our discretionary spending is too high. It all starts when we notice a few dollars left over each month, so we get a cat, join a gym, sign up for a two-year Verizon phone contract, or get sucked into an "awesome" two-year Direct TV deal. None of these expenses are mandatory. They should be things we can drop at any time if a hardship comes: a job loss, medical condition that prevents us from working, family medical emergency, etc. If we don't keep these in our minds as discretionary, the next thing we know, these discretionary things have become mandatory, and we just can't seem to make ends meet. We can't afford those nice gifts at Christmas and can't watch Monday night football on ESPN. This takes discipline, and this takes a budget.

> *Proverbs 21:20 – There is treasure to be desired and oil in the dwelling of the wise; but a foolish man spendeth it up.*

This passage tells us not to spend our money foolishly. We should instead carefully consider where we spend our money and should pray about large purchases and commitments, such as signing a contract for a new auto loan, a new house, cable TV, or a cell phone provider.

> *Proverbs 21:5 – The thoughts of the diligent tend only to plenteousness; but of every one that is hasty only to want.*

If we make hasty decisions with our money or decide to not live by a budget, we will wonder at the end of each month where the money went. *Why don't I have anything left?*

> *1 Corinthians 16:2 – Upon the first day of the week let every one of you lay by him in store, as God hath prospered him, that there be no gatherings when I come.*

Caution on Debt

I hope you can see that if we live paycheck to paycheck or, worse, spend more than we make, we get ourselves into trouble quickly. We should avoid borrowing at all costs. Borrowing and investing are opposites of one another. In the case of borrowing, you are paying the money you owe plus interest. In the case of investing, you allow others to borrow your money, and they pay you back with interest. It sounds simple: Investing is better than borrowing. God even commanded the Israelites not to borrow but to be lenders.

> *Deuteronomy 15:6 – For the LORD thy God blesseth thee, as he promised thee: and thou shalt lend unto many nations, but thou shalt not borrow; and thou shalt reign over many nations, but they shall not reign over thee.*

*Deuteronomy 28:12–13 – The L*ORD *shall open unto thee his good treasure, the heaven to give the rain unto thy land in his season, and to bless all the work of thine hand: and thou shalt lend unto many nations, and thou shalt not borrow.* [13]*And the L*ORD *shall make thee the head, and not the tail; and thou shalt be above only, and thou shalt not be beneath; if that thou hearken unto the commandments of the L*ORD *thy God, which I command thee this day, to observe and to do them:*

Furthermore, the book of Proverbs tells us not to lend money (be surety) to anyone (which includes co-signing loans):

Proverbs 11:15 – He that is surety for a stranger shall smart for it: and he that hateth suretiship is sure.

Proverbs 17:18 – A man void of understanding striketh hands, and becometh surety in the presence of his friend.

Let's look at an example of a budget based on all we have learned to see this in practice. I currently live outside of Baltimore, MD; therefore, the numbers below are based on a married family with two incomes. Since this is a book on godly marriage, the budget is for a couple.

Incomes and expenses will vary greatly, so I used a variety of websites to estimate the averages, including USDA for groceries, Baltimore Gas & Electric (BGE) for utilities, AAA for auto expenses, etc. Your income or expenses may be different, but this will illustrate the point we are trying to make about savings and living within your budget. Notice in this budget, there is no debt/other. We assume this person owns a car, but he paid for it rather than take out a loan and is not carrying any credit card debt. Because of this, the family is also able to save their 10% liquid savings and have money left to invest as well as spend money on a variety of discretionary activities. However, if, like most people in America, they take out a loan to buy a car and carry a monthly balance on their credit card, we can see the impact clearly in the next table.

Foundational Needs

Category	%	Monthly Budget Amount	Comments
INCOME:			
Wages/Income Net		$3,651	In Baltimore Avg after tax income $3651
Interest Income		$232	
INCOME SUBTOTAL		$3,883	
Mandatory EXPENSES (72-90):			
Tithe (10)	10%	$388	
Rent/Mortgage (30)	25%	$978	Inc. Homeowner's fees / 2 roommates
Utilities - Heat (5-10)	4%	$135	Water + BGE - based on average $135
Groceries/Food (5-15)	6%	$233	USDA (low-mod) spending
Debt/Other (5-10)			
Medical (2)	2%	$78	co-pay, glasses, dental work
Auto Maintenance & Repairs (3)	10%	$377	AAA avg 15k miles/annual 60.8 cents/mile
Ins: Medical (8)	5%	$183	Avg: Ind $183 - Family $414
Ins: Auto (2)	5%	$183	Avg 30yo $2200/year
Ins: Home (2)	1%	$34	Avg Annual MD $824 split in two
Discretionary EXPENSES (5-10%):			
Entertainment + Shopping	2%	$78	Movies, sporting events, etc.
Dining Out	2%	$78	
Utilities - Discretionary	3%	$116	Internet + Phone + Cable
Clothing/Drycleaning	3%	$116	
Miscellaneous Items	4%	$155	Gifts, Vacations, Gym Membership, Pets
EXPENSES SUBTOTAL	81%	$2,978	
Investment & Savings (5-10%):			
Savings	10%	$388	Liquid
Investment/Retirement	5%	$194	
SUBTOTAL	15%	$ 582	
NET INCOME			
(Income – Expenses)		$ 323	

Category	%	Monthly Budget Amount	Comments
INCOME:			
Wages/Income Net		$3,651	In Baltimore Avg after tax income $3651
Interest Income		$0	
INCOME SUBTOTAL		$3,651	
Mandatory EXPENSES:			
Tithe	10%	$365	
Rent/Mortgage (30)	27%	$978	Inc. Homeowner's fees / 2 roommates
Utilities - Heat (5-10)	4%	$135	Water + BGE - based on average $135
Groceries/Food (5-15)	6%	$233	USDA 3 people (low-mod) adj 1 person
Debt/Other (5-10)	27%	$977	Avg used car loan $352 / Avg CC $625
Medical (2)	2%	$73	co-pay, glasses, dental work
Auto Maintenance & Repairs (3)	10%	$377	AAA avg 15k miles/annual 60.8 cents/mile
Ins: Medical (8)	5%	$183	Avg: Ind $183 - Family $414
Ins: Auto (2)	5%	$183	Avg 30yo $2200/year
Ins: Home (2)	1%	$34	Avg Annual MD $824 split in two
Discretionary EXPENSES (5-10%):			
Entertainment + Shopping	0%	$0	Movies, sporting events, etc.
Dining Out	0%	$0	
Utilities - Discretionary	3%	$110	Internet + Phone + Cable
Clothing/Drycleaning	0%	$0	
Miscellaneous Items	0%	$0	Gifts, Vacations, Gym Membership, Pets
EXPENSES SUBTOTAL	100%	$3,648	
Investment & Savings (5-10%):			
Savings			Liquid
Investment/Retirement			
SUBTOTAL	0%	$ -	
NET INCOME			
(Income–Expenses)		$ 3	

The story is much different now. This is a typical budget of many Americans today. Again, this information is based on averages of what a typical household carries for car loans and credit card debt. Look what happens to this average family. They have no money

132

left for investments, and they have very little money for discretionary spending.

This is what I mean when I say a family is living beyond their means; this budget is ultimately unsustainable and unrealistic. As the monthly credit card debt goes up, this family will need to cut back on mandatory spending by living in a smaller house, using less heat, and eating less. It's also unrealistic to live without discretionary spending. We can discipline ourselves to not do certain "cool things" for a while, but eventually we start looking at other people and think, *Well, they have a new cell phone, They go to the movies,* or *They eat out with their friends.* Then we feel pressure to do the same, and we supplement our mandatory spending with credit; that keeps our bills going up each month, and we are constantly behind.

This is called "keeping up with the Joneses," or the fleshly desire to have. That one-time frivolous expense of a fancy dinner out will only be fun for the few hours that someone is engaged in it, but when the pain of paying for that dinner comes due month after month, it may not seem worth the small amount of fun that lasted a very brief time.

When the bill comes due, this causes stress on the family. The husband and wife fight over finances and what they "really" can afford, and this may begin to rip them apart. Why? Because there is an underlying fear that foundational needs cannot be met due to indiscriminate spending.

A budget will help you tell your money where to go and keep you on track with your spending so that it doesn't get out of control. It's an accountability tool. I encourage newly engaged and all married couples to discuss and set spending limits through the use of a budget and then to track their expenditures against their budget so that they can ensure those basic needs are met. It will truly help them have peace in their marriage.

Cheri's Story

Desperate to be independent, I moved in with my first husband after only six weeks of knowing him. I didn't really have the money to move out of my parents' house yet, but there was no rationalizing with me then. We didn't create a budget, so we were doomed and didn't realize it. We both had stable jobs with a decent salary at the time, but we did not live within our means. If we wanted something, we charged it. We got married after living together for three years. We moved to new jobs with bigger salaries and bought a larger house, better cars, and nicer vacations but still did not live within our means. I realized after a couple years of living this way, and a few years after having our son, that we needed to reduce our spending and plan for the future. My ex-husband didn't have this epiphany. He gained his happiness from having things and always lived in the moment. In addition to not having a budget and having to charge discretionary expenses, we didn't discuss major purchases. I found myself afraid to open the mail for fear of another "late" notice. I began to lose trust in him as a protector and provider. Although I doubled my salary by working a job in northern Virginia (commuting from north of Baltimore), we still had enormous amounts of debt and zero in our savings account. As our marriage began to crumble, I thought about putting a little money in my own savings account because I knew I needed to protect myself. When we officially divorced, I walked away with more than $30K just in credit card debt. This didn't include the car loans and the mortgage we had together.

Fast forward to 2005 when I married Eric. Every time a bill came in the mail, I would hand it to Eric and then hover over him like a helicopter waiting for him to pay it. He wasn't happy that I questioned his ability to provide and protect, and I wasn't at peace because of the lack of trust I had with my ex. Eric created a budget for our new blended family, which included paying off my credit card debt from my first marriage. He put us on an allowance for our discretionary purchases, and he enforced this budget. In

13 years of marriage, I haven't had to play helicopter wife each month when the bills are due because I know he is protecting our foundational needs. I no longer worry about our finances because he guided our family to a strong financial status free of debt.

Financial Needs vs. Financial Wants

As a teenager, I joined the U.S. Navy. All of my foundational needs were provided by the Navy. When I was hungry, I went to the galley; when I was tired, I would lay down in my rack. There were no mandatory expenses, no rent, and no food to buy, and they even provided me with clothes (a uniform) to wear. All the money I made was uncommitted and used as discretionary funds. After taxes, I made less than $800 a month. It didn't take long for me to spend that money.

At first, I was happy with what the Navy provided. It was good to have freedom and be out on my own, even if I had to eat cafeteria-style food and sleep in a large room with 50 other guys. As time went on, I was offered the opportunity to live off base and receive a housing allowance. The Navy gave me an extra $400 to pay for rent and food per month. It was an exciting opportunity to have a better living environment and better food to eat. In the local paper, I found a roommate who would split a $600 per month, two-bedroom apartment. After my share of the rent, I had enough left over to buy food, so I agreed. I forgot to consider how I would get to work. I didn't have a car, and I couldn't afford much. I managed to find a car for about $5,000 with loan payments of $100/month. What I didn't consider was gas, insurance, title, tags, registration, etc.

All of a sudden that $1,200 a month wasn't going as far as it used to go. Now I had all these new mandatory expenses. After rent, a car payment, gas, and food, I only had a few hundred dollars left. However, I continued to spend my money like I still had $800 of discretionary funds. At the beginning of the month, I was spending like normal, and the latter half of the month I was eating less food, was going out less often, and kept wondering what had happened to all my money.

After four years in the military, I was honorably discharged and took a job working at the Navy base as a civilian contractor. Due to my Navy experience, I was making $10 an hour. This was $300 a month more in take-home pay. I was now back to almost $800 a month in discretionary spending. So what did I do? After several bad roommate experiences, I decided it was time to live on my own. Getting a one-bedroom apartment doubled my rent and actually ended up reducing my discretionary spending.

Two years later I was promoted to a shift supervisor position with a pay increase to $13 an hour. Now I was making an additional $400 a month. I could certainly live comfortably. After all, I was able to live on very little before. But no! I grew into my new income. After having unreliable transportation and unpredictable repairs that would sap all my discretionary income, I decided I needed a new car—not a more reliable car, not a car with fewer miles but a BRAND NEW car! Even cars that are well maintained and kept in pristine condition decrease in value over time. On average, a new car depreciates in value by at least 10% as soon as you drive it off the lot.[14]

The point is we can easily blur the line between wants and desires. I didn't need to live on my own; I could have found another roommate. I definitely didn't need a new car—maybe a better, more reliable car but certainly not a new one. This scenario is very common to most of us. We get a bump in pay, and the next thing we know, we are scratching our heads and asking where all our money went. We must be careful not to blur the lines between wants, desires, and needs.

Safety, sustenance, and shelter are needs. A want is a desire, and it typically starts as a need but raises the bar in quality: new versus used car, lobster versus chicken, Starbucks coffee versus homebrewed Folgers. We all make a thousand decisions a day, and

---

14 *https://www.nerdwallet.com/blog/loans/compare-costs-buying-new-car-vs-used/*

if we don't treat God's money seriously, we will easily get caught up in spending more than we have on wants versus needs. We need to make sure our incomes can support the wants we have, and if not, we need to spend our money on our needs first. Our desire should only be for what is attainable within our budget.

The Debt Deception

After my first son, Matthew, was born, my budget needed to include a new mouth to feed, daycare expenses, and additional clothing for him. At first his mother and I lived together, but within two years, we eventually went to court, and I was paying child support of close to $600 a month. This wiped out nearly all of my discretionary spending. What I should have done was reduce my mandatory expenses by selling my car or getting a roommate, but I didn't want to go backward in my life. I was used to the way I was living and didn't want to sacrifice, so I fell into a trap. I used credit cards to supplement my income. This is when I started to live beyond my means. I spent more than I made and started down a slippery slope.

I started buying things on credit, which left more money in my pocket and made me believe I had more available income to spend. However, it was all an illusion. I really didn't have that extra money. In reality, I could spend each dollar once, but when I borrowed, I was trying to spend the same dollar twice. One dollar on the credit card left a dollar in my pocket to eventually go toward something else.

God had provided for me economically, but rather than reduce my spending, I misspent what God had already provided for me and my family. If I had just honored him with all of my spending, I would not have been in that bad situation. When the credit card bills came due, I reduced or stopped tithing altogether just to make my debt payments. I remember thinking, *If I just had some more money, I would tithe.* But God had provided me with more money in the past five years. I had gotten two significant increases in my pay, but rather than thinking of my income as God's money, I thought of it as my money. We need to submit our purchases in prayer to him. If I had done that, I would have certainly sold my car to be able to continue tithing. In essence, my car became more important to me than God. This is what God was talking about in Exodus 20:3:

Thou shalt have no other gods before me.

About a year later I had some debt, and I still wasn't tithing, but I was able to make my monthly credit card payment. Then a bad storm caused a big tree branch to fall on my new car, scratching my paint, shattering my windows, and causing more than $5,000 in damages. I called the insurance company, and they said this was under the category of "acts of God." These types of damages are covered by an optional piece of insurance that I didn't purchase because I needed to save money. Instead of paying another $20 on my car insurance, I now had to pay more than $5,000 to repair my car. I never prayed about what to do. I just decided to max my credit card to pay for that emergency expense. If I had been saving money, I would have been able to pay for this from savings, but instead, I plunged myself further into debt.

Debt limits our freedom. Being in debt diminished my ability to recover from that accident. I was barely able to afford my way of living before the accident. Now this surprise expense really set me back financially.

James 4:14 – Whereas ye know not what shall be on the morrow. For what is your life? It is even a vapour, that appeareth for a little time, and then vanisheth away.

This passage tells us tomorrow isn't guaranteed. Nor do we know what tomorrow will hold for us. We don't know if we will have a job that allows us to pay our debts. Shortly after that accident, I was laid off, and I had to rush into the first offer of employment I had because I was in debt and couldn't afford to take my time to search for the right job.

When my church took a special offering for a needy family, I couldn't support it. The debt I was in robbed me of the blessings of God. God wanted me to use his money to take care of my needs and to be a blessing to this needy family, but because I spent his money selfishly, I was robbing myself of the blessings God had in store for me.

When we borrow money, we become slaves to those that we borrow from:

> Proverbs 22:7 – The rich ruleth over the poor, and the borrower is servant to the lender.

Serving God first in all things is paramount to the Christian life. However, when we borrow money, sometimes serving God and those we borrow from can be in conflict. We can start to become more of a slave to our lender and not to God.

If we continue to borrow, debt takes more and more prominence in our lives, to the point where it's almost insurmountable. We may want to do what God wants, but we no longer have the financial means to support God's direction in our lives. We start getting calls from debt collectors, and now we have a different master. Debt becomes an obstacle between you and what God wants you to be in your life.

Getting Out of Debt

Now that we have discussed the dangers of debt and how to live within our means, perhaps you are reading this and thinking, *I am already in debt. Now what do I do?* There are four steps to getting out of debt biblically:

1. <u>Prayer</u>: Start with telling God you weren't a good steward of his money, and let him know you are ready to change. Not only will God help you stop accumulating debt but as you eliminate debt, God will bless your faithfulness.

2. <u>Don't accumulate new debt</u>: To eliminate debt, we need

to be serious about not getting back into debt. Sometimes people start to pay down debt and get to a place where their debt goes from crushing to just uncomfortable, and then they buy some new thing on credit. They think they have it under control. If we really have a change in perspective on debt, we should eliminate the word "loan" from our vocabulary.

Gaining weight and gaining debt are similar. It takes a lot longer to lose it than to gain it. A friend of mine was 50 pounds overweight. He was traveling a lot for work, eating fast food all the time, and started to put on weight little by little until one day he was at the doctor's and they told him he had high blood pressure. It was so bad he needed to start taking medication. It was a wakeup call, and he was disgusted with his condition. He decided he was going to do something about it that wouldn't involve medication.

He made some radical changes. For almost a year, he didn't eat high-fat sweets, he only drank water, and he started counting calories. Not only was his weight down but his blood pressure was too. It took a radical change in his thinking to make a transformation, just like getting out of debt. We need to make big changes if we want to see big results.

Perhaps it's turning off the cable bill, getting rid of the cell phone, eliminating eating out, or trading in the car we have for a more affordable one (Luke 12:15). Those are luxuries, not necessities. Changing our financial status takes work to cut out excess spending and requires radical changes in our attitudes and in our actions.

Proverbs 6:4–6 – ⁴Give not sleep to thine eyes, nor slumber to thine eyelids. ⁵ Deliver thyself as a roe from the hand of the hunter, and as a bird from the hand of the fowler. ⁶ Go to the ant, thou sluggard; consider her ways, and be wise:

We need to get busy if there is work to be done. If you are in debt, you have work to do. God calls us to action to fix the situation immediately. Just like a deer, when they hear a hunter, they don't just stand there; they run. Don't sleep (v. 4) and don't stand still (v. 5) but move! We need to work hard like ants (v. 6) till we are out of debt. Get busy like ants, and run from the debt you've accumulated so you are no longer the servant to the lender (Proverbs 22:7).

3. <u>Get to work</u>: One way to stop from spending money is to earn money. Take a second job if you have the available time, and it will keep you busy. You won't have idle time to spend money on things you desire.

4. <u>Establish and stick to your budget</u>: A budget is a communication tool for husbands and wives to agree on where the money goes. Faithfulness and stewardship require planning, and a budget keeps one another accountable. I would recommend you meet daily or weekly to discuss expenses. Eventually it may only be necessary monthly.

According to Zillo, the median home price in Maryland is about $325,000. Most people need 10 years to make that kind of money. Imagine having saved up that money and you decided to build a house. How would you build it? Would you just hand all your money to the builder and say, "Build a two-story house with three bedrooms and a bathroom"? No, you would want blueprints, plans, inspections, etc. You might want to check out a model home to see it in person. You would be very involved in the planning because spending that kind of money is important. However, many of us will accumulate that amount of debt in our lives, and we do it without thinking, without planning, and without our spouse being involved.

Tithing was first mentioned in Genesis 14 during the time of Abraham. Long ago, before the law was handed down to Moses in the 10 commandments, the tithe (the law) required giving 10%. Some think we are not under the law, we are under Christ, and they are correct, but doesn't grace require more than the law? I can do a whole lot more with 90% of my income and God than I can do with 100% on my own. God honors those who honor him (1 Samuel 2:30).

Create a budget as a couple, and get serious about tracking the money God has blessed you with. It honors God when we plan. A budget isn't about the husband dictating to the wife or vice versa. It is about two partners agreeing on the financial planning for the family together.

Budgets will change over time, so revisit them every so often. As your family grows and changes, your budget should grow and change too.

Stick to the plan. It takes five to seven months of following and tweaking a budget before a family will get into the rhythm of using it properly. Don't get discouraged if it doesn't work right away. Be flexible and cooperative. If you and your spouse feel you need more for groceries, discuss it and adjust if necessary, but don't overcorrect either. Don't get alarmed when you overspend dining out by 10% by overcompensating and reducing it to 2%. Just stick to it; then re-evaluate monthly at first and less frequently after you have a good rhythm.

5. Be accountable: By using a budget and monitoring expenses, you can hold each other accountable to what you agreed upon and start living within your means. A budget means nothing if you don't pulse check your finances once in a

while to see how well you are doing against the budget. Be honest with your spouse about what you spend so that trust and transparency aren't affected.

As you start to be faithful with little things, don't be surprised when God starts to give you more finances to manage. Your debt will be eliminated if you follow your budget. The effects will snowball, and when people get intentional about paying off their debts, they will typically do it ahead of plan.

PUTTING OUR MONEY IN GOD'S HANDS

When Cheri shared the difference between me and her first husband, my ability to manage had nothing to do with my wisdom or knowledge. I learned how to budget because my past mistakes in managing money forced me to budget. I was at a point in my life financially where I knew I needed to make a change, and I couldn't have done it without the strength of God to help me. I give God the credit for our financial blessings and my ability to protect and provide.

Our foundational needs of shelter, safety, and sustenance are provided by the money we earn. If we have a proper biblical view of money, we can provide for our foundational needs and our tithes and have more peace in our marriages.

Recently I chose to leave a job and took two months finding a new job. I had enough savings to pay for six months of mandatory expenses. Knowing I could pay our bills gave me and my wife peace and allowed God to direct my path through thoughtful prayer toward the exact opportunity God had intended for me to have:

Philippians 4:6–7 – ⁶Be careful for nothing; but in every thing by prayer and supplication with thanksgiving let your requests be made known unto God. ⁷And the peace of God, which passeth all understanding, shall keep your hearts and minds through Christ Jesus.

When we do all things through prayer and supplication, God will direct our paths, leading to good results and peace in our lives. Being debt free, budgeting, and tracking where we spend our money allows God to bless us and, through us, bless others with our finances.

6

LEGACY NEEDS

A legacy is what people leave behind for future generations. It's how others remember that person and evaluate the impact they had on their life. If someone has lived their life for God, when that life is over, God will say, "Well done, good and faithful servant… enter thou into the joy of thy lord" (Matt. 25:21). Everyone was put on this earth for a God-given purpose (Rom. 8:29–30). When Jesus came to stand before Pilate, he told Pilate that he had a purpose:

> *John 18:37 – Pilate therefore said unto him, Art thou a king then? Jesus answered, Thou sayest that I am a king. <u>To this end was I born, and for this cause came I into the world</u>, that I should bear witness unto the truth. Every one that is of the truth heareth my voice.*

Jesus had a God-given purpose for being placed here, and he was motivated to see that purpose achieved and to honor God with his life on Earth. A Christian's legacy should be to pursue a God-given purpose and to honor God with their living. When Christians do what they are designed to do, their spirit is engaged, and they are excited and motivated because they are fulfilling their purpose.

When Christians are doing something other than what they are designed to do, they end up unmotivated and frustrated, and they may not put in the effort they should. Therefore, it is imperative that Christians discover what God's purpose is for their lives and then get busy performing that purpose. When that purpose is completed, that will define their legacy.

It took me nearly 40 years to find my God-given purpose in life. For 40 years, God was shaping me to be used to fulfill that purpose. The natural talents I was born with, the classroom training I acquired, and the trials I suffered all shaped who I am today. I now understand the greatest purpose in life is not to pursue happiness. I understand that the trials in my life helped me to mature, and now I accept those trials with a more positive attitude. The trials in my life have brought me closer to God, have helped me to counsel other couples from a unique point of view, and have led me to ultimately serve other people that are hurting too.

> *1 Peter 4:12–13 – *[12]*Beloved, think it not strange concerning the fiery trial which is to try you, as though some strange thing happened unto you: *[13]*But rejoice, inasmuch as ye are partakers of Christ's sufferings; that, when his glory shall be revealed, ye may be glad also with exceeding joy.*

Trials will produce joy in our lives. We don't realize it at first, but after we are through the trial is when we see the glory of Jesus revealed. Those trials lasted for years: When my son was born out of wedlock and I only saw him once a month, when I was in court fighting to see my children, and when I was in a loveless marriage, I was miserable! I was miserable because I didn't have God in my life. Now, after more than 13 years of being married to someone I adore, having a strong relationship with God, and serving in a ministry today, I understand the reasons for those trials, and I use them to help others avoid or navigate through the same mistakes I've made. My poor choices resulted in misery, but the misery led me to Christ. Praise the Lord!

At the age of 16, I was saved. It was Christmas, and I was traveling from my dad's house in Buffalo to my mom's house in Pennsylvania. During that trip, I met someone who was attending Bible college, and he showed me in the Bible how I was not worthy of heaven and that only by placing my faith in Christ and what He did on the cross would I be able to get to heaven. It was that day that I discovered I needed Jesus in my life. However, I didn't start living my life for Jesus. I selfishly wanted Jesus to save me but wasn't ready to give up my worldly living. As my life continued to cause me pain and anguish, I would begin to turn to God. He was important to me, but I didn't attend church regularly.

After my son was born, I started attending church on a more consistent basis. I would go to church at least a couple Sundays a month, but I didn't attend Sunday school classes nor was I connected to the people in the church. Church made me feel better when I was down. I would run to the church to help "lift my spirits" and would feel better but still didn't read my Bible regularly or pray daily. I treated God like a magic genie and would call out to him in my pain, but when things turned around and were going well, I was less likely to pray, read my Bible, or attend church.

After my divorce, I ran back to church and dove in headfirst. I finally realized that living my life without God only led to ongoing disappointment. This was a clarifying moment in my life when I realized the only happy moments I had in my life were when God was a part of it. Now I was in church and more dedicated and focused on having God in my life, but it still wasn't clear what my purpose was. Being in church taught me about Jesus, encouraged me to have a relationship with Jesus daily, and helped me to identify the areas of my life that needed improvement. Living for God required me to be saved and to conform to the image of Jesus Christ (Romans 8:29). The more I attended church, the more I read my Bible and the clearer I could see where my life needed improvement. The Bible instructed me and corrected me to be a better person by relying on the Spirit of God to guide me. That is when I started to realize and fulfill my God-given purpose.

A few years after I started attending church regularly (yes, I was a slow learner), I began to realize that ultimately God wanted me to do two things: to help spread the truth of the gospel and to help those that are part of our church family. This is my purpose, my ministry. In order to do that, I needed to seek God first in EVERYTHING! This was contrary to how I had lived my life up to that point. I was usually selfish, never content with my circumstances, and focused on my needs and not the needs of others. Is it any wonder my life was miserable? Now I consider others before myself, and I bring ALL my decisions to God. The friends I keep, the decisions I make, and every thought are brought before God in prayer (2 Cor. 10:5). Ministry is when we serve, mentor, and encourage others (1 Peter 4:10–11) and when we give hope to those that are hurting (Rev. 21:4). This life is not about promotions, not about buying more stuff, and not about pleasing ourselves. The Christian life is about your ministry, and it should be impactful to others around you. It's using the Spirit of God to reach the children of God with the message of God.

WHAT IS MY GIFT?

God gave everyone certain gifts and talents at birth, whether they are the gift to teach and preach, the gift to sing, the gift of being organized, the gift to lead and manage, the gift of charisma, etc. No matter what gifts or talents they have, God gave those talents to his children for the sole purpose of glorifying him with those gifts. 1 Corinthians 12 discusses various spiritual gifts:

> *¹Now concerning spiritual gifts, brethren, I would not have you ignorant...⁴Now there are diversities of gifts, but the same Spirit.*

Christianity is not a spectator sport; everyone should inventory their God-given talents and discover what God intended for them to do with those talents.

If you are a great singer but choose not to use your talent as a singer in service to God, there will always be a void in your life. Perhaps you choose to pursue a career path that doesn't include singing. This void will cause you to feel less motivated to perform the career path you have chosen, and if you persist in that career, you will feel more frustrated in your life. We are designed by God to fulfill a specific purpose in our lives, and when we choose to live our lives outside of that God-given role, the role we choose becomes less fulfilling. Part of our Christian walk should be to discover the purpose that God made us to fulfill. It could be a career as a songwriter, or it could also be to raise children in the nurture and admonition of the Lord (Eph. 6:4). Whatever we are designed to do, we need to ensure we are using those God-given talents to honor and glorify God.

I wish I could tell you specifically what God intended for you to do, but God made us a diverse people. He made each of us different and with different talents; however, we all serve the same goal, which is to glorify God. In the Bible, 1 Corinthians 12 emphasizes that we all have different talents but are to use them toward a common goal:

> *1 Corinthians 12:11-14 – [11]But all these worketh that one and the selfsame Spirit, dividing to every man severally as he will. [12]For as the body is one, and hath many members, and all the members of that one body, being many, are one body: so also is Christ. [13]For by one Spirit are we all baptized into one body, whether we be Jews or Gentiles, whether we be bond or free; and have been all made to drink into one Spirit. [14]For the body is not one member, but many.*

Unity is therefore key to serving God as a collective people. Notice that verse 12 says we are "one body" and verse 13 says we are "one Spirit." The reason it is important to be Spirit led is because when we yield to the Holy Spirit, we are all working in unity toward a common, God-directed goal.

A legacy is what you leave behind when you are finally called to heaven. What will people remember about you? What impact will you have on others? I sure want God to say, "Well done, good and faithful servant...enter thou into the joy of thy lord" (Matt. 25:21). Our legacy should be to pursue life goals that honor God.

MARRIAGE AND OUR LEGACY

Before we get married, we need to ensure that our God-given purpose, our legacy, is complementary with that of our future spouse. I could meet the perfect person for me, but if God is taking us in two completely different places in our lives, then it's not going to work. We need a spouse that is willing to support our life choices that honor God.

Many people that I interviewed during the research phase of this book told me that they ended up divorced because their spouse did not support their dreams and aspirations. This can take the form of a career decision (to be a pastor or engineer) or a non-career decision (to serve in a ministry or on the PTA). If what we love to do can help make money for our family, that is truly a blessing, but that is not always God's purpose for our lives.

One person I spoke to was dating someone from the same college. Both people were doing religious studies and had a desire to do God's will with their lives, and as their college years went on, one of them was being called into the mission field in Asia, and the other felt a calling to pastor a local church near their hometown, which wasn't in Asia. Uh...Houston, we have a problem! These two people quickly realized that their lifelong ambitions, God's calling for their lives, obviously didn't allow them both to serve together, so they broke up. This may seem sad, but it is much better than having one of them give up God's will for their life and to feel frustrated, unmotivated, and resentful. This situation could have potentially led them to despise their future spouse many years later.

Frustration and conflict in a marriage could be caused by one person pursuing their calling while the other person is having to settle. It should seem obvious that if God is calling two people to pursue life choices that are in conflict with one another, then God did not intend for those two to be a couple.

OUR LEGACY AFTER MARRIAGE

Sometimes we don't know what God's will is in our lives before we get married, or perhaps it changes over time. What do you do when you are already married and then a life choice comes along? Well, first we must pray about it and seek God's direction through the Holy Spirit.

Our choices after marriage should not only be discussed with God but with each other too. Our spouse should be involved in every decision that will impact them and the family. We need to be sure that our choices are not disobedient to God and that they are agreeable to and supported by our spouse.

A married couple should mutually agree to what is best for the family through the Spirit. Sometimes we can put so much pressure on our spouse that they will "give in" to our request, or in some cases, we make decisions and don't consult our spouse. In those cases, the person making the decision may be getting what they want, but it has caused distance in the relationship. The spouse that decides to make a big decision like quitting their job, deciding to move, or making a major purchase (e.g., new car) without discussing it will make the other person feel as if their opinion doesn't matter, and this can result in feeling a lack of love, causing this couple to begin to drift apart. Our need to pursue our purpose in life should be encouraged by our spouses or we may feel unloved. Although we may feel that getting what we wanted gives us joy, we certainly don't have peace in our marriages or our homes. Eventually robbing us of the joy we may have once felt from initially getting our way.

Cheri's Story

When my son was not quite two years old, a company from northern Virginia reached out to me and offered me a job making twice my salary. I have to admit to this day that it was quite flattering to get that offer. When I told my ex-husband about the job offer, he was ecstatic. I was not. My immediate reaction was "No way can I be away from my baby boy for 12 hours a day, five days a week and with such a stressful commute. We just talked about trying for a second child." While he was focused on the financial gain, I was stressed at the thought of not being able to be a mother to my baby boy. Being a mother was a role that I had always dreamed of—a job that was the most important job I ever wanted! The role of mother was far more important to me than my role in the working world.

I can remember the night as if it were yesterday. My ex-husband was excited for this job, where he said we would pay down debt and help our family financially. His exact words were "You need to sacrifice your own happiness for the welfare of the family." With those words haunting my every thought, I reluctantly accepted the job. Just when my son was turning two years old, just when we would grow our family, and just when I was happy, I boarded a train on the northern side of Baltimore at 5:20 a.m., arrived in DC at 6:40, took two metro trains to Arlington, VA, and walked seven blocks to my building. After being awake for three hours, I finally sat down at my desk to begin my day's work at 7:30. I worked until 3:30 and then did the same thing in reverse, arriving at my car at 5:45 each night. Sometimes my ex would still be at work, so I would pick up my son from daycare. I was one of the last parents to pick up their child, and the guilt destroyed me.

When we got home, I would make my son dinner and sit with him while he ate, talking to him, staring at him, and just missing him. I didn't make dinner very often for my ex-husband because I was too exhausted and he was usually still at work, so family dinner time was non-existent. After my son ate, I'd give him his bath, and then we'd play together for about 30 minutes until it was time for him to go to bed at 8 p.m. I would read to him in bed, where most nights I would fall asleep beside him, breathing in the smell of a freshly bathed child and holding him as close as I could. Typically, by 10 p.m., my ex would come in and wake me up, and I'd pack my lunch, set out my clothes for the next day, and fall into bed, where I think I was asleep before my head hit the pillow.

This was not much of a life. Not much of a family. Not much of a marriage.

Our marriage, although we didn't really know it at the time, was broken. Financial stress wasn't really a concern anymore. Oh, we actually had accrued MORE debt and still lived beyond our means, but the financial stress was replaced by relational stress. Combine the stress of being away from home for 13 hours a day with the fact that we had undergone infertility treatment and then suffered a miscarriage. I felt that my purpose was to be a mother, a good mother, yet I couldn't fulfill that purpose.

I don't believe I ever really communicated my unhappiness adequately to my ex-husband. I recall telling him how I hated the commute, hated being away from our child, and hated that I couldn't be a stay-at-home mom, but I don't think he understood nor did I truly explain why. I was frustrated and lonely and then became bitter and angry. The little time we had on weekends or weeknights to possibly be a couple or a family, I only focused on my child, not my marriage. I was angry at my ex for making me take a job I didn't want and not allowing me to be a mother. His casual disregard for my need to be a mother crushed me to the inner core. I hated *money* and *things* and found myself emotionally abandoning the marriage. Just over two years after taking that job, we were separated. Our marriage was over, our family broken. My son would never know what it was like to have both his parents in one home.

Neglecting Legacy Needs

When we neglect the legacy needs of our spouses, we not only feel frustrated and unmotivated because our heart is elsewhere but we also start to feel distance from our spouse and at times angry or resentful, much like Cheri felt when her ex-husband was not satisfying her legacy needs to be a mother to her son. She wanted to raise their son and felt like her working career was getting in the way of her being the kind of mother she wanted to be. On the other hand, maybe her ex-husband was frustrated because he felt like he wasn't providing adequately for his family financially; therefore the foundational needs couldn't be met if she chose the lower-income job, so her ex-husband didn't support the legacy of his wife.

If I had an opportunity to counsel them, I would have told them to first of all live within their means. Your lifestyle must support your legacy needs. God did not put us on Earth to live luxurious lifestyles or keep up with the Joneses. He did put us here for a reason, however, and we must yield to the direction of the Holy Spirit to fulfill our purposes. In other words, God will never jeopardize our foundational needs of shelter, food, and clothing to fulfill his purpose. His calling in our lives will complement our foundational needs so long as we decide to live within those means.

My wife and I recently were given an opportunity to go to Israel with our pastor and some other church members. This was a great opportunity to learn more about Christ in the context of where it all happened. I initially was thinking this trip would have helped my teachings in the Sunday school class by giving more context to the people I was ministering to, but it would have cost us nearly $10,000. After praying about the decision for many days, I eventually didn't get the feeling that God was calling us to go on this trip. It would have been a financial hardship for the family, and there was no way I could manipulate our budget to afford the trip; therefore we didn't go. If God had wanted us to go, he would have provided the resources. He would have made a way for our budget to make sense. In the future, our church would like to plan another trip to Israel, and now we are in a better position to afford this extravagance. God's timing is perfect, and if we listen to the leading of the Holy Spirit, we will be sure to be blessed and peaceful in our lives and marriages.

Spouses need to support the legacy needs of each other. We need to yield to the Holy Spirit, find our purposes, and fulfill these purposes in our lives. Whether they are career goals or personal goals doesn't matter as long as they are God's goals for our lives. We need to not only figure out God's will for our lives, but if we plan to marry, we need to understand God's direction in the lives of our future spouses. Many marriages are pulled apart because of a spouse that doesn't support the other's legacy needs. When we are supportive of our spouses' legacy needs, our spouses will feel loved, and it will bring peace and joy into our marriages.

WHAT IS GOD'S WILL FOR MY LIFE?

Solomon had all the resources he could think of to chase down every option in life in order to seek fulfillment. He had all the wealth, all the knowledge, all the pleasures of life, and all the possessions, and yet he called it all vanity of vanities:

Ecclesiastes 1:2 – Vanity of vanities, saith the Preacher, vanity of vanities; all is vanity.

Solomon was the wisest man to ever live. He was a wise ruler until he started taking multiple wives (more than 700 plus 300 concubines). Some of these wives were ungodly women that started to turn Solomon's heart from the Lord and caused him to worship idols and even sacrifice his own children to false gods. In Ecclesiastes, Solomon asked more than 30 questions, all surrounding the topic of "What's the point of life?" At some point in our lives, we probably all ask that question. We may have pondered the direction our lives will take us or how we know what success is. Do you wake up, go to work, come home, eat dinner, watch TV, go to bed, and then do it all again the next day? God gave you a greater purpose than that.

When you go on a road trip, don't you usually have an endpoint in mind? A national park? A beach? A friend's house? And to figure out how to get there, isn't it a lot easier to do that when you've mapped it out? If you know where you want your life to go, it's a lot easier to make a plan to get there. I'm not sure what your target is today, but I hope it's not just a bigger paycheck or a nicer house. We should be trying to figure out why God put us here on Earth and what his plan is for our lives. Our goal in life should be to seek and understand why God created us. Rest assured, there is a purpose, and it isn't just to get more stuff, to attain a higher social status, or to do things for ourselves. If you go through life just thinking about what you can get out of it rather than what you can put into it, you will end up like Solomon, calling it all vanity or emptiness.

I worked for the same company for 17 years. This was where I met Cheri. This was the company that paid for my master's degree. This was the company that basically helped me grow from a junior cyber security engineer to a leader in the industry. I was loyal to this company, and I assumed I would stay there until I retired. But things changed with the vision and integrity of the company, and the way they conducted business did not align with my own personal core values. I began to complain about the job, something that Cheri didn't really hear me do. I began to complain about my boss. I began losing sleep and losing weight because of the stress it was causing. Whenever Cheri would try to talk to me about it, I just told her that this was just a stumbling block and it would all work out over time. She gave me more time, but things didn't improve; they got worse. My health was now impacted, and so was my relationship with Cheri and our boys. I didn't want to get up in the morning, and I didn't want to go to work with people I no longer respected. I was miserable. I felt this loyalty to them though. How could I leave after 17 years?

Cheri finally had a heart to heart with me. She told me to quit without finding another job first. She said that my health and happiness and our relationship were more important than our house and the stuff in it. We would sell the house and downsize if it meant I was happy. This was difficult because I thought my purpose in life was to help our nation's security by being a cyber security expert. I had to pray long and hard over this decision. I wasn't getting the feeling that God wanted me to leave this company, yet he was closing that door and opening new ones. So I finally did it. I quit. By the grace of God, I found a new job, a better job, a few days after I started looking. We didn't have to sell our home either. In fact, after careful review of our finances and cutting back on a few things, I was able to take time off between jobs to dedicate my time and focus on finishing this book.

I truly believe that writing this book was God's plan for me and for Cheri—to help others understand the dangers of having a marriage without God and to understand God's design for marriage as well as to articulate the struggles Cheri and I went through without God and how much more unified and loving a marriage can be when God is a part of it. Leaving my job was scary, but it was an act of faith that God had better plans, and he did! When we follow God's plan, he makes a way for things to work out better than we can even imagine (Ephesians 3:20).

We should have a reason, a God-given purpose, that motivates us to get out of bed in the morning. Otherwise, we live a vapid existence. Our lives are just empty and without purpose. If you don't know why God put you here, it will be like running on a treadmill: You keep running but just don't seem to be getting anywhere.

Going back to the book of Ecclesiastes and Solomon's endless questions about life, he next describes life as an endless cycle that never seems to do anything:

Ecclesiastes 1:4–7 – ⁴One generation passeth away, and another generation cometh: but the earth abideth for ever. ⁵The sun also ariseth, and the sun goeth down, and hasteth to his place where he arose. ⁶The wind goeth toward the south, and turneth about unto the north; it whirleth about continually, and the wind returneth again according to his circuits. ⁷All the rivers run into the sea; yet the sea is not full; unto the place from whence the rivers come, thither they return again.

He says in verse 4 that people come and go but the earth is still here, the sun rises and sets, the wind blows continually, and the rivers dump into the sea and never fill it. This is like our lives when we get up, go to work, come home, eat, and go to bed day after day, never really achieving anything. You run the "rat race" without making any real progress.

How much money would be enough? How high up the corporate ladder is high enough? What salary would you need to make to be content with the pay that you have? If you don't understand the point of life, you will always be going after more, more, more.

Ever spend hours working on a document or something on the computer and then you lose power and, by association, lose all the work you've done? You panic, you spend time searching for the latest saved version, and you may pound your fists on the keyboard, but unfortunately, it's gone. It's that way with your life when you aren't doing the will of God with your life. It's all pointless if the world is the same when you leave it as it was before you arrived.

When you're living life for you, lust of the flesh, lust of the eyes, and pride of life, it means nothing. Unless you are doing God's will, you will not have an impact in this life, and you will never be truly happy. If you aren't serving God with your life, helping others, and making an impact, then it's like losing that document you worked hours and hours on. Poof! All for nothing.

A legacy is leaving the world better than when you found it by making an impact, a difference! You can't make a God-driven impact without Jesus Christ living through you. If all you're doing is aimlessly wandering, it's pointless.

Solomon, in his own flesh, was trying to satisfy himself, and he found life was vanity (empty) and pointless, without meaning. He wasn't doing the will of God. But we serve a God who is in the restoration business. He can transform us and change us. If you are living in the flesh, it may seem hopeless and pointless, but when you live for Christ and when you discover your purpose in Christ, you can find meaning and direction and have clear goals.

FOLLOWING GOD'S WILL

If you follow the will of the Lord, you are wise. You will figure out your purpose, and you will discover meaning in your life.

> *Ephesians 5:17 – Wherefore be ye not unwise, but understanding what the will of the Lord is.*

On this road trip we call life, it's a lot easier if you know where you're going and if you know God's will. God created us for *his* plans. Cheri and I have a pillow in our living room that says, "If you want to hear God laugh, tell Him your plans." It makes you stop and think, doesn't it? The creator of the universe probably looks at us and chuckles when we come up with our approach to finding happiness and think we have it all figured out.

Many people start out life asking, "What do I want to do? What will make *me* happy?" Although we do need to enjoy what we do for a living, it's not just about us. We need to be asking, "What will make *God* happy? What does *God* have planned for my life?"

> *Jeremiah 1:5 – Before I formed thee in the belly I knew thee; and before thou camest forth out of the womb I <u>sanctified</u> thee,*

Sanctified means to be set apart and made holy. Holy is just another way of saying *used of God*. Before you were born, before you took your first breath, God had a holy purpose for you. You are here with a unique set of skills to perform a specific godly purpose, and if you don't fulfill that purpose in your life, your life will seem empty and pointless.

Do you have a talent or skill that comes easily to you? Perhaps you are good with finances. Is that just so you can buy a better house and better car? Or is there a more spiritual purpose for that gift? If you aren't sure what you are here to do, what your purpose in life is, then perhaps it's time to look at a few aspects of your life. We each need to evaluate our skills. We need to look at our past experiences and our passions to see what God might have built us to do:

Ephesians 2:10 – For we are his workmanship, created in Christ Jesus unto good works, which God hath before ordained that we should walk in them.

Ephesians 2:10 tells us God "ordained" us to do "good works." God made each of us with specific abilities and skills, so we ought to use them to glorify him and serve others. Glorifying God and loving others are the two great commandments found in Matthew 22:37–39.

I started speaking in public when I was in the Navy over 25 years ago. I never imagined that the talent and skill God gave me would be used in my career and then eventually lead me to teach a Sunday school class. Our skills and our natural abilities help mold our purpose. Not only did God give me a skill for speaking publicly but he also gave me a passion to learn and to teach others. God created Cheri with a passion for people. He gave her the gift of compassion to love people of all walks of life, to help them and make them feel accepted. He also gave her the gift of discernment to be able to sense when something may be wrong even when someone isn't sharing. Somehow she is able to get to the heart of the matter and make them feel better about whatever they are going through.

We have faced trials that we brought upon ourselves that God is now using to help others who are going through similar struggles. We weave our stories into the way we teach and counsel. Again, praise the Lord for the lessons he taught us!

Cheri and I have complementary gifts that we are using for a singular purpose to glorify God. Through all those years of pain that we went through, separate from one another, he brought us together for HIS greater good. WE are better than ME. God had a specific audience in mind when he put Cheri and me together. By myself, I could have taught a class or even counseled others, but it wouldn't have been as effective without Cheri's gifts of compassion and discernment. Alone, Cheri could have counseled and helped others, but she says that she may not have been as effective without my ability to analyze and simplify God's Word to be more understandable and applicable.

Some of us may say we are so broken that we can't be used of God, that our past is our past and we made too many mistakes. Nothing can be further from the truth. There is nothing God can't redeem if we let him. We must live in the moment, using the past to make better future decisions. There are plenty of examples in the Bible of those who thought they were unable to be used of God and went on to do great things. Moses, David, and Peter, just to name a few, all failed, but God restored them and used them in a great way. When we are at our weakest is when God can do great things!

When I look back at all the decisions we've made and all the God-given abilities we have, it is now clear to me that God called us to be together and serve in a ministry together helping soon-to-be and married couples. We feel God is calling us to use our past pains of divorce to help those thinking of marriage to do it right from the start and to help struggling marriages thrive again. If Cheri and I can share our past with others and help them avoid mistakes we've made, then we believe we are fulfilling God's purpose for our lives. We never have more joy or satisfaction than when we're helping others have a stronger relationship with Jesus Christ, which, in turn, improves their relationships with one another.

Following God's plan for your life may not mean you have to quit your job, sell your house, and join the mission field. It happens one step at a time.

Psalm 119:105 – Thy word is a lamp unto my feet, and a light unto my path.

To follow God's will, you don't need to have your entire life planned out. You just need to take it one step and one decision at a time and submit major decisions in prayer. God doesn't always reveal his plan for your entire life. Typically, he tells us how to take one step at a time. "A lamp unto my feet" means we are focused on the very next step we will take, not the next three steps or even two steps, just the next step. We have to watch where that light on our feet is shining and take one step at a time, in God's direction.

You have to ask yourself if you are doing what brings *you* pleasure or what brings *God* pleasure.

Revelation 4:11 - For thou hast created all things, and for thy pleasure they are and were created.

This life should not be about what we can get out of it but how we can please the Lord. When you have a close relationship with God, then it will become clear what will please Him. And what pleases Him will please you. We were not created by God just to follow our own selfish pursuits. We have a job here. We have a mission. We have some purpose for our existence, and we have a legacy. What we do in life should be bringing God joy and pleasing him. When we start to pray about every decision to use our talents, skills, and past experiences to help others, we please God. We need to walk with God day by day and subject those decisions and those steps we will take to please Him.

7

WHAT IS MARRIAGE?

Being an introvert, I do enjoy my alone time, but nothing gives me greater joy than when my wife and boys are with me. God designed us to live in families and not to be alone. All families ought to start from marriages, and God clearly tells us what marriage is in Genesis 2:

> [18]And the LORD God said, It is **not good that the man should be alone**; I will make him an help meet for him.[19]And out of the ground the LORD God formed every beast of the field, and every fowl of the air; and brought them unto Adam to see what he would call them: and whatsoever Adam called every living creature, that was the name thereof. [20]And Adam gave names to all cattle, and to the fowl of the air, and to every beast of the field; but for Adam there was not found an help meet for him. [21]And the LORD God caused a deep sleep to fall upon Adam, and he slept: and he took one of his ribs, and closed up the flesh instead thereof; [22]And the rib, which the LORD God had taken from man, made he a woman, and brought her unto the man. [23]And Adam said, This is now bone of my bones, and flesh of my flesh: she shall be called Woman, because she was taken out of Man. [24]Therefore shall **a**

man leave his father and his mother, and shall cleave unto his wife: and they shall be one flesh.

There are three important observations about marriage in this passage.

OBSERVATION 1: ADAM SHOULD NOT BE ALONE

We all need relationships, and God emphasized this in Genesis 2:18 when he said, "It is not good that the man should be alone." Imagine Adam in the Garden of Eden. It was a perfect place. He had all the animals and all the fruits and sustenance he could want, but he was still alone. It doesn't matter how much we possess in life; the constant feeling of loneliness is not good, it causes harm, and it damages our psyches and our physical health. One of the harshest punishments in our penal system, apart from capital punishment, is "solitary confinement"—isolation from other prisoners. Solitary confinement is cruel because it removes all communication with others, and it deprives the inmates of relationships. God did not create us to be alone. God created us to be together with other people.

First, in verse 20, after God saw that Adam should not be alone, He created for him a "help meet." God created Eve to *help* Adam, to be the mirror image of him, yet with different gifts and attributes. In a marriage, we are supposed to help each other the way God intended for Eve to help Adam.

God created Adam and Eve as the first family.

OBSERVATION 2: TWO BECOME ONE FLESH

The second observation is that two become one flesh (v. 24). One flesh implies that when one is hurting in a marriage, the other is hurting too; when one of us celebrates victory, we both celebrate victory.

Marriage is a strong bond between two people. In a marriage, we make a covenant before God. This is more than a contract; it's a life-long commitment. In my first marriage, I did not understand this concept at all. My motivation to get married the first time wasn't based on a committed, loving action; it was a naive, worldly, and selfish decision that I thought would make the best of a bad situation. It was based on the pressures of my family and society. It was selfishly motivated by "looking good" in the eyes of others and "making my life easier".

From the moment of my proposal, we started to discuss the *contract* of our marriage: how our household would operate and who would be responsible for what. We discussed finances and divided our bills equally. She paid for "her" car, and I paid for "my" car. We discussed chores: I'll do the dishes if you cook the meals. I'll drop our son off at daycare, and you pick him up. The marriage was two people cohabitating together. Our lives became a list of expectations and responsibilities. The family existed only because a child was born. It never had trust, it barely had love, and we entered into it for all the wrong reasons.

Initially, we treated each other well because it was the right thing to do. When the dilapidation began when someone shirked their responsibilities, disappointment entered into the relationship. We stopped meeting each other's needs. One day I knew she needed to talk to me, but I just didn't feel like it. I had had a hard day and thought I deserved to relax, so instead, I flopped on the sofa and ignored her basic need of communication. Slowly but surely, she didn't want to talk to me, she never wanted to do things with me anymore, and we stopped being intimate. Eventually we were sleeping in separate beds and just existing in the same house together, each in our own little world. I felt like she wasn't living up to her end of the contract, so neither would I. If she wasn't going to be nice to me, then I was not going to be nice to her. Sarcastic comments and rude behavior started to become the norm between us. We would fight or just live with the tension in the house. But the problem is that this type of attitude just caused our relationship to be even more miserable. We both were angry and frustrated at one another yet not willing to change.

Out of sheer stubbornness and pride, I would not admit the relationship was failing. I didn't want other people to see yet another failure in my life. I endured the misery of the tension and frustration. Some days were stressful and others were quite depressing, but I hung on. Once in a while, I would see my ex-wife act more committed to the relationship. She would treat me well, or we had a special bonding moment with Ryan. This glimmer of hope would incentivize me to do more for her and things would recover, but the relationship never got to the heights of our "best days." Those were behind us, never to be seen again.

This is the existence under a contract marriage. When I said the traditional vows at the altar, I viewed them as ancient words repeated vainly without thought. Neither of us truly understood those words let alone lived by those words. How could we when we didn't really place God as the authority of our lives?

Contracts are made in the business world all the time and clearly define the mutual benefit each party receives. In those contracts, we have clauses that allow us to break the contract should the mutual benefit no longer exist. Most people today treat marriages like a contract. When one party stops providing the benefit, the other party wants to break the contract and end that relationship.

A biblical marriage is a covenant. A biblical marriage says that we will continue to do our part, to love each other, and to meet their needs regardless of what we get from this relationship. It is a promise. It says I will not take this lightly and I will continue to participate in this relationship regardless of the consequences I receive. The traditional vows state "in sickness and in health, for richer or for poorer, for better or worse." Unfortunately, many of us fail to meet our commitment (vows) when there is sickness, financial struggles, or the dilapidation phase.

Today, my marriage to Cheri is a covenant, a commitment. I knew going into the relationship that I wanted to make her happy, that I wanted to take care of her. The relationship wasn't a chore; it was a privilege. We never negotiated who would pay what bills; we have shared our finances from the very beginning. We didn't argue over chores; we just did what needed to be done, and it naturally worked out. I try very hard each day to wake up and think about what I can do to make my wife happy. She is the first person I want to see in the morning and the last person I want to see each night.

I was traveling for my job about two to three times a month, and when I did, I was a little depressed. I would call her each morning and talk to her each night before bed, but it wasn't the same without her there. Even when we suffered through our dilapidation and stagnation phases, I still knew it was imperative to show and remind Cheri that I loved her, especially when there were stressful times. Of course, some days I'm better than others. I may not always meet her needs, but I am aware of what to do when things go sideways. Unlike in years past, with God's power, I now bounce back from my selfish actions much more quickly. By understanding how God loves us, I can show Cheri how I love her. I show her love *every* day, not always because I "conditionally" feel like it but because I vowed to love her, and I plan to keep that commitment.

The covenant I have with my wife is like God's covenant with us. God loves us unconditionally. These four points talk about how God loves us:

- We love God because he first loved us. (1 John 4:19)
- He will provide all our needs. (Phil. 4:19)
- We are one body united with God through Jesus Christ. (Rom. 12:5, 1 Cor. 6:17, John 6:44)
- God will never leave you nor forsake you. (Heb. 13:5)

These points and supporting Bible verses tell us that we are unified with God and that God shows his love toward us by meeting our needs. God will never turn his back on us despite how we treat him. God has a covenant with us that he is incapable of breaking. Our covenant relationship with God should be the model we use in our marriages.

As Christians, when we have Christ living *in* us, it is then that we are <u>one body and one flesh</u> with God through Jesus Christ. When we are one flesh with God, we should not fight against our own body (God). When my physical body needs water, I don't deprive myself of that need; I quench my thirst. I meet that need to make my body healthy.

In the covenant of marriage (one body, one flesh), when my wife needs me to talk to her about something, regardless of how tired I am, I need to give her my attention. My desire may be to flop on the couch and be in my own world, but I can't do that. If I ignore her need to connect with me, it deprives my wife of the attention she desires. Giving her what she needs is feeding the marriage (the body) and making it healthier. A covenant puts the needs of our spouses before our own.

The covenant of marriage is not about my needs; it's about the needs of my spouse. Being one body and one flesh is a strong marriage concept that needs to be taken seriously. The relationship that comes closest to this is children. When our kids misbehave and disappoint us, we don't stop taking care of them. When our boys were younger and they misbehaved, they would be punished, but we would still feed them dinner. They needed to eat, so we wouldn't deprive them of satisfying the body's need to be fed. We love our children unconditionally. Unfortunately, we have a tendency in our marriages to treat our spouses conditionally (more like a contract), and we withhold meeting the needs of our spouses because they disappoint us. This hurts the marriage, and it hurts the body.

Observation 3: Leave Then Cleave

Finally, the Bible tells us that not only does a man cleave (stick to, adhere) to his wife and become one flesh but he also leaves his father and mother. When a young man and young woman join together in marriage, they leave their parents behind. They are still part of the <u>natural</u> family, but their marriage family takes priority. Many marriages suffer because the parents of the new husband or wife interfere into their kid's relationship. Cheri talks to her mom almost every day. I understand the bond they have. It's okay for Cheri to ask for her mom's advice about marriage in general, but if Cheri started telling her mom all the ways in which I disappointed her, then it would become an issue. Wives need to stick up for their husbands, and husbands need to stick up for their wives. They are now of the same flesh, and a married couple should not allow their parents and other family members to have a negative influence in the relationship.

When we vent to family members and complain about our spouses, they tend to hold onto these offenses, and they bring up the past hurt over and over again, long after we have forgiven our spouses. This makes it harder for us to truly forgive our spouses when we are reminded of their pasts. From that point forward, our families will judge every action of our spouses and always view them with a critical eye.

Another issue some couples struggle with is letting the parents influence decisions that should remain between spouses, such as rearing children or finances. Once you are married, family discussions no longer involve the parents; it should be between the husband and wife to jointly decide. If a young husband and wife want to seek wisdom from their parents, they should both decide to do so with mutual consent and have that discussion all together.

Our spouses are one flesh with us and are therefore more important than <u>any</u> other relationship besides our relationship with God. We leave our parents and cleave to our spouse. Cleave means to stick, to adhere, and to hold to. We need to stick by our spouses, not vent to others. We need to stick with each other. The natural family becomes secondary to the marriage family.

THE NEED FOR ROMANCE

All marriages need romance and physical intimacy. Have you ever wondered what the Bible says about sexual relations or physical intimacy? It's pretty simple. First, the Bible tells us that it is only allowed within the confines of marriage. Secondly, the Bible forbids fornication (physical intimacy with unmarried people) and adultery (physical intimacy with married people).

> *Hebrews 13:4 – Marriage is honourable in all, and the bed undefiled: but whoremongers and adulterers God will judge.*

> *1 Corinthians 6:18–20 – [18]Flee fornication. Every sin that a man doeth is without the body; but he that committeth fornication sinneth against his own body. [19]What? know ye not that your body is the temple of the Holy Ghost [which is] in you, which ye have of God, and ye are not your own? [20]For ye are bought with a price: therefore glorify God in your body, and in your spirit, which are God's.*

The Bible also tells us to be fruitful and multiply. After God used a flood to destroy all of mankind except Noah and his family, he commanded them to "replenish the earth."

> *Genesis 9:1 – And God blessed Noah and his sons, and said unto them, Be fruitful, and multiply, and replenish the earth.*

In addition to a married couple procreating, the Bible tells us that physical intimacy is for pleasure. There is one book in the Bible that discusses romance and physical intimacy in depth, the Song of Solomon (SOS). I've done a deep dive into this book that is often avoided due to some fairly intense romantic words; we shouldn't be embarrassed if we are using God's Word as guidance for a healthy physical relationship with our spouses.

The Song of Solomon follows one couple from dating to the wedding and into their marriage. This book of the Bible can be dissected into three sections that cover the phases of their relationship:

dating (chapters 1–2), the wedding (chapters 3–4), and the marriage (chapters 5–8). The five aspects of romance (purity, pursuit, compliments, courtship, and physical intimacy) are found throughout each phase of a relationship. Every one of these needs is absolutely required in marriage.

The Need for Purity

A critical element to romance is purity. In the SOS, the couple saves themselves for marriage and are both very aware of their own temptations. During the wedding, the man refers to his spouse's purity poetically by comparing her to a closed garden, a shut spring, and a sealed fountain.

> *Song of Solomon 4:12 – A garden inclosed is my sister, my spouse; a spring shut up, a fountain sealed.*

In SOS 2:1, the woman refers to herself as the "lily of the valleys." Lilies are white flowers that symbolize purity throughout the Bible. After the wedding, the husband refers to his wife as "my undefiled" (SOS 5:2, 6:9).

Another aspect of purity is faithfulness. While dating, the woman says, "My beloved is mine, and I am his" (SOS 2:16). This was to represent the purity before marriage and their dedication and commitment to remain faithful to each other. After the wedding, we see this same statement repeated twice, emphasizing its importance (SOS 6:3, 7:10). When we are married, we need to remain faithful to one another, and our spouses should be the <u>only one</u> we desire.

> *Song of Solomon 7:10 – I am my beloved's, and his desire is toward me.*

This passage demonstrates the faithfulness and desire this married couple has maintained.

Chapter 2 of Song of Solomon also shows this couple keeping their distance from one another to maintain their purity:

Song of Solomon 2:14-17 – ¹⁴O my dove, that art in the clefts of the rock, in the secret places of the stairs, let me see thy countenance, let me hear thy voice; for sweet is thy voice, and thy countenance is comely. ¹⁵Take us the foxes, the little foxes, that spoil the vines: for our vines have tender grapes. ¹⁶My beloved is mine, and I am his: he feedeth among the lilies. ¹⁷Until the day break, and the shadows flee away, turn, my beloved, and be thou like a roe or a young hart upon the mountains of Bether.

The man calls out to the woman he is dating, "O my dove…let me see thy countenance, let me hear thy voice…." He desires her and calls to her, and she responds with a warning of foxes spoiling the vine and tells him to "flee away." This passage can be interpreted to mean let's keep our distance so as to remain pure. We need to be careful of the devil and draw closer to Jesus and the Word of God. When baby foxes eat of a vine, they will literally destroy it. Foxes are cunning and crafty animals that destroy what they eat, just like the devil is cunning and crafty and wants to destroy our purity with desire. In verse 16, the woman says her man is "feeding among the lilies." We said before that the lily in the Bible is symbolic of purity and is also symbolic of Jesus Christ. "The Word was God" (John 1:1), and if we are "feeding on meat of the Word of God" (John 6:27), we can repel the temptations of the devil.

The Need for Pursuit

Our desire for our spouses should make us want to pursue them even after we are married. Before marriage, pursuit is natural. We are competing for the affections of our husbands and wives to be among all the other potential companions. Therefore, we must be actively pursuing and wooing our future spouses. The pursuit ultimately ends with a proposal in the Song of Solomon (3:1–4). In chapter 1, the woman is asking where her man is: "Tell me… where thou feedest" (SOS 1:7). It was common for shepherds to take breaks in the middle of the day when the sun was hottest. She is inquiring where her man is because she wants to spend time with him. In chapter 2, the man was so excited to see her that he was "skipping upon the hills," and he was calling to her to come away with him (SOS 2:8–15). These two were so in love that they were pursuing each other with earnest.

After the wedding, he calls her away to journey from Lebanon to the mountains (SOS 4:8). This was like a honeymoon. They took a trip away together after their wedding.

After the wedding, they continued to pursue one another. He comes to her while she is sleeping and she doesn't immediately respond, so he leaves. By the time she gets up to see her husband he has left (SOS 5:1-8). She searched for him and calls for him, exclaiming "return" four times in the same verse (SOS 6:13).

It is easier to be romantic while dating, but after our wedding we need to consciously keep the fire alive through romantic gestures. When we become partners (helpmates), after the wedding we tend to become busy with life (careers, housework, children, etc.). We have a tendency to stop *wooing* each other and not trying as hard as we once did to pursue our spouse. By continuing to meet those romantic needs <u>after</u> the wedding, we keep our spouses desire focused on us and this protects our marriage.

The Need for Compliments

The man and woman in Song of Solomon are constantly showering each other with compliments. While dating, they both make it known that the other is the best among all possible marriage prospects:

> *Song of Solomon 2:2–3 – ²As the lily among thorns, so is my love among the daughters. ³As the apple tree among the trees of the wood, so is my beloved among the sons. I sat down under his shadow with great delight, and his fruit was sweet to my taste.*

While comparing her to all other women, he calls her "the lily among thorns" (SOS 2:2), and she calls him an "apple tree among the trees of the woods" (SOS 2:3). She goes on to say he provides protection ("I sat down under his shadow") and provision ("his fruit was sweet to my taste"). He tells her she is fair and comely (very attractive) multiple times (SOS 1:10,15–16; 2:14). After the marriage, he compliments her from head to bosom (SOS 4:1–7) and later from feet to head (SOS 7:1–7). The wife praises the husband (SOS 5:10–16), and the husband praises the wife (SOS 6:4–7).

Our spouses will always want to seek and receive our approval and our desire for them. We must consciously give compliments to confirm our love for them.

The Need for Courtship

Courtship is defined as "the act of wooing in love,"[15] and is an archaic term used to describe dating that usually ends with solicitation of a woman to marry. Courting can include wearing nice clothes, using perfume or cologne, displaying our best manners, and taking the time to set the scene for dates. These are the actions we take to gain the attention of our future spouses. In the Song of Solomon, we see the woman adorning herself with jewelry before the marriage (1:10) and during the wedding (4:9).

The sense of smell is an important aspect to romance. Many studies have proven that certain scents can trigger powerful emotional responses. These studies show that basil, cinnamon, and citrus flavors aid in relaxation, whereas peppermint, thyme, and rosemary help to energize. Ginger, cardamom, licorice, and chocolate have been reported to arouse a sense of romance. Specific aromas have been proven to improve productivity, relieve stress, comfort hospital patients, and increase cognitive functioning. Indoor aroma technology has been used by many successful businesses, including Monte Carlo and Bally's Resort Hotels, select Marriott hotels, Dunkin Donuts, Starbucks, Mrs. Fields Cookies, and Walt Disney World, and has had a positive effect on sales.[16]

In the Song of Solomon, smells are used to set the scene for romance (1:12–14,17; 3:6–11; 7:12–13). Various scents are

---

15 http://webstersdictionary1828.com/Dictionary/courtship
16 Hunter, B. T. (1995, 10). The Sales Appeal Of Scents. *Consumers' Research Magazine*, *78*, 8.

mentioned, including myrrh, frankincense, spikenard (balsam), camphire (henna flower), cedar, aloes, grapes, pomegranates, mandrake, saffron, calamus, and cinnamon. All were pleasant smells that produced powerful emotions, the same way businesses use them today to influence shoppers or improve productivity.

The man and woman, throughout the various phases of their relationship, make the effort to set the stage. Courtship comes naturally when we are dating. We want to impress our spouse-to-be, and we go out of our way to do so. We take the time to plan the perfect date and to surprise them with things that make them feel extra special.

The Need for Physical Intimacy

Physical intimacy is more than just sexual relations. In chapter 1 of the Song of Solomon, the woman talks about her man laying against her bosom (v. 13) and later how he embraces her (2:6). Romance includes physical touches that are non-sexual. Holding hands, sitting side by side, and putting your arm around your spouse are all ways to be romantic. The woman desires not only to be embraced but to be kissed (SOS 1:2). They exclaim that love is better than wine (SOS 1:2,4; 4:10).

The important thing to note is that these various physical encounters were all predicated on their purity and proceeded by the other aspects of romance, including compliments, pursuit, and courtship. The entire process is important to men and women. A man feels close to his wife *after* they have been physically intimate, and when wives feel close to their husbands, they have the desire *to be* physically intimate.

The moments of physical intimacy are poetically described during the wedding (SOS 4:10–16) and then again later after they are married (SOS 7:6–8,12–13). During the wedding, this intimate moment is what we call consummating the marriage. When we hear the phrase "consummate the marriage," we know it means that two people had sexual intimacy with one another after they exchanged vows. The word consummate means to end, to finish by completing what was intended.[17] This definition indicates that a marriage is not complete without intercourse. The last part of the wedding day is to cleave (to unite or be united closely in interest or affection; to adhere with strong attachment[18]) with our spouses.

When two people cleave to one another, first they do it as a covenant by exchanging vows, swearing before God and witnesses that they will put their spouses' needs above their own, no matter what. Second, they may celebrate with a dinner or reception. Finally, after they are joined together legally and publicly, they will join together or cleave physically. They consummate the marriage and complete the union.

Marriage is the only proper construct in which to express sexual feelings with another person. When two people join together physically, it forever changes them. From that point forward, a piece of you is connected to the other person. It is irreversible. The object illustration I like to use is that when you mix and mold together yellow Play-Doh with blue Play-Doh, you get green Play-Doh. Can you make those pieces become separate blue and yellow chunks of Play-Doh again? No, because they are physically connected; they have cleaved to one another and can never be separated. I can make two chunks of green but never one yellow and one blue again.

It's the same with people. God meant marriage to work in a manner where two become one flesh. He designed sexual relations to be the glue that connects two people so intimately that no one can separate them. That includes not sleeping together before marriage. Your virginity is the best gift you can ever give your spouse. That is why fornication (sex before marriage) and adultery (sex outside the marriage) are sins. When we are intimate outside of marriage, we are damaging ourselves physically as well as psychologically.

When we are intimate, we connect emotionally and physically, and if a relationship ends, we actually pull those two things apart,

17 http://webstersdictionary1828.com/Dictionary/consummate
18 http://webstersdictionary1828.com/Dictionary/cleave

creating a wound in the heart; that is scar tissue. Scar tissue is dead skin with no nerve endings; it cannot feel. When you continue to have multiple sex partners, you tend to develop metaphorical "scar" tissue on your heart that makes your heart cold and unfeeling. Ultimately, having multiple sex partners makes it challenging to have a healthy marriage or sexual relationship. The devil turns something God wants to use in a special way and perverts it to hurt us physically and emotionally. God knew how we were supposed to function as human beings, and his plan will bring the ultimate happiness to our marriages if we just follow his direction. This includes not sleeping together before marriage. Marriage is the only safe, God-ordained institution in which to properly express sexual feelings. Back to the Play-Doh example: If I keep combining different colors of Play-Doh together, eventually I end up with a dark, gray lump. That is analogous to the condition of our hearts; we damage our psyches each and every time we have sexual relationships that end.

I was a virgin when I graduated from high school, even though my parents never taught me to save myself for marriage; they taught me to be cautious. It was pretty much a green light for me to have sex outside of marriage. School also taught me to be cautious. Anyone in school could get condoms from the school nurse with no questions asked. Since age 14, the authority figures in my life were telling me, "It's okay; just use caution." From that point on, I always thought having sex outside of marriage was okay.

Fast forward four years later. It was the summer before I left to join the U.S. Navy. I'd gotten myself into a situation where I was faced with the decision to have sex. All kinds of emotions and thoughts were swirling in my mind. I was terrified and exhilarated at the same time. In the back of my head, all I could hear was "It's okay; just use protection." My fleshly desires and what the world taught me justified my actions of going through with it. I never looked at this girl the same way again. From that moment on, we had a special bond. The experience cemented us together. We made plans to keep seeing each other until a few weeks later, when I left for boot camp. She wrote me letters at first, but over time, she stopped.

For the first time in my life, I was heartbroken over the ending of a relationship. This was different than when I just stopped being friends with someone. It led me into a depression that I never escaped from until I met that next special girl. Then my only thought was, *When will we be intimate? When will I be able to feel that special feeling again?* But again, that relationship failed, and heartache set in until I found a new girlfriend. Eventually meaningful relationships became one-night stands, and sexually intimacy was never as special as it had once been. I took a precious gift from God and cheapened it into something mediocre.

A sexually satisfying marriage is important. When we say, "I do," we are committing to our spouse physically too. Each person should be meeting their spouse's sexual needs, and their level of intimacy is an important aspect to a healthy marriage and should be considered one of the relational needs we need to fulfill in one another. Remember, God commanded us to have healthy sexual relations since the beginning of time. He told us to "be fruitful and multiply" (Gen. 9:7) to populate the world. God wanted children born within a marriage, and to do so requires a fulfilling sexual relationship with your spouse.

The problem with some marriages today is that men just want to be physically intimate with their wives but don't want to meet their wives romantic needs. They don't want to spend the time and effort to be romantic (dress nice, put on cologne, make dinner reservations, have non-sexual intimacy such as embracing and holding hands). All these things are romantic gestures that women need to feel closer to their husbands and to therefore desire physical intimacy. Romance starts at the beginning of the day and, if done right, can end with physical intimacy. Just like other loving actions, we need to purposely make romance a priority over other things in our lives (kids, work, housework, etc.)

There was a time in our marriage when Cheri thought she had "lost her libido." This happened around the same time she had a hysterectomy, and it was easy to blame it on biology. In fact, many studies support this conclusion, but what both of us discovered was that her hysterectomy had nothing to do with her lost libido. This all took place during our stagnation phase. There was clearly a distance between us. She didn't feel emotionally close and therefore wasn't interested in being physically close. I stopped doing those romantic things, and at times, I was being a real jerk to her. As our relationship started to recover and I started meeting her needs again, our love life improved.

Just as the Song of Solomon illustrates what we did at the beginning of a relationship, we need to keep doing those things even after we are married. Being romantic requires effort and planning, and those loving actions help produce the loving feelings and maintain the unity in our marriages.

AM I READY FOR MARRIAGE?

Now that you know the marital needs maybe you are wondering if you are ready for marriage. People have often asked me, "How long should I date? When do I know it's time to get married?" There is no definitive timeline, but I answer their questions by giving them a list of things they should be doing before making the decision to marry:

1. Create a deep relationship with the Lord.
2. Serve in a ministry.
3. Validate their character.

Create a Deep Relationship with the Lord

To be ready for a thriving, godly marriage, you must first have a relationship with God that makes you feel whole. We each must be whole as individuals before we decide we want to be married. A healthy relationship with the Lord should be first and foremost in our minds every day. No one can possibly serve the needs of others without having the proper heart attitude for God. Matthew 6:31–34 says:

> [31] *Therefore take no thought, saying, What shall we eat? or, What shall we drink? or, Wherewithal shall we be clothed?* [32] *(For after all these things do the Gentiles seek:) for your heavenly Father knoweth that ye have need of all these things.* [33] *But seek ye first the kingdom of God, and his righteousness; and all these things shall be added unto you.* [34] *Take therefore no thought for the morrow: for the morrow shall take thought for the things of itself. Sufficient unto the day is the evil thereof.*

In short, this passage says to seek first the kingdom of God. Seek God first each and every day, and all your needs will be satisfied. If we don't have God, we can't have our needs satisfied on Earth. Christ is the key to filling all that our hearts desire. Ephesians 1 tells us:

> [22] *And hath put all things under his feet, and gave him to be the head over all things to the church,* [23] *Which is his body, the fulness of him that filleth all in all.*

Jesus Christ fills us with everything we need (all in all). What does he fill us with? The Holy Spirit. When we are filled with the Holy Spirit, we start to spread that love toward others. When we are filled with God's love, we can easily give agape love to others. That is why Bible reading, church attendance, and prayer time are essential to the Christian's health. We need to fill our spiritual tanks every day because the circumstances of this world will try to empty those tanks. It's why the Bible tells us to pray without ceasing (1 Thess. 5:17) and "give us this day our daily bread" (Matt. 6:11).

Serve in a Ministry

Filling our spiritual tanks and having a proper relationship with God helps us to serve in a ministry. Every Christian should have a ministry they serve in. Whether it's providing child care, working in security, bringing doughnuts to Sunday school class, or being a church greeter, we all have some service we could be doing for others. Serving others is important because it teaches us about agape love: to give of ourselves and expect nothing in return. We should serve in a ministry *before* we get married because this prepares us for the ministry of marriage.

When I was in the Navy, we practiced fire drills over and over and over again. The reason behind the need for "drills" is that if a fire breaks out on a ship in the middle of the ocean, you have nowhere to run. You basically <u>must</u> fight that fire successfully or die. So we would practice fire drills until our responses became automatic. We didn't panic when the real fire came, because our minds were almost on autopilot. We relied on muscle memory and instinct that had been drilled into us. By seeking God daily and serving in a church ministry, we are practicing a fire drill for marriage. Practicing how to give while expecting nothing in return, to be joyful with bitter people, to have patience with angry people, or to defuse conflict with love will equip us to handle those inevitable situations in marriage. Our muscle memory will kick in, and our marriage will be thriving and peaceful marriages.

Ephesians 5 is often used during sermons about the responsibilities of the husband and wife:

> [22]*Wives, submit yourselves unto your own husbands, as unto the Lord....*[25]*Husbands, love your wives, even as Christ also loved the church, and gave himself for it;*

Many couples may have a hard time hearing this, let alone executing these commandments from the Bible. If we obey God, then we have practiced submission, and if we have been serving in ministry, then we have practiced agape love, just like Christ has for us, for his people, for the church. You see, these commands are not difficult to follow when we are *all* following Ephesians 5:21: "Submitting yourselves one to another in the fear of God." By practicing love in our ministries, we are practicing for the ministry of marriage. Making the decision whether to marry should not be a stressful decision if you have been obeying the Lord.

Validate Their Character

Hopefully you have been trying to grow your own personal relationship with God, so the person you want to marry should be doing the same thing. Before we get married, we should be seeking God to help make us whole. We should not be looking for a spouse to "complete us." We first need to be satisfied and accepting of who we are. To be complete by ourselves requires Jesus, who makes us whole (Eph. 1:23). So what you seek in a spouse should be the same thing you are trying to develop personally in yourself.

You also want to make sure they are participating in a ministry. You must make sure they understand love and submission before agreeing to marry. Anyone struggling in their relationship with Jesus will certainly not be able to fill your needs in a marriage. They are still trying to get their own needs fulfilled, and until they have a personal, ongoing relationship with Jesus, they won't understand how to love.

If they do have a strong relationship with Jesus but haven't practiced how to love in a ministry, they certainly won't be giving you the love you need in a marriage. You don't want your marriage to be *practice* for a loving relationship. Back to my Navy days and the fire drills: If we had one untrained person with us when a fire broke out, we may have faced some challenges. We may have succeeded, but it wouldn't have been as effective as having an entire team participate in the fire drills that was well trained.

While you are dating, you should validate the character of your potential spouse. How do they treat their family, their friends, and strangers? If they are disrespectful to the waitress in a restaurant, that may say a lot about them. How they look at and value other people says a lot about how they may value and treat you. A common saying that my mother used to always tell me was "You can fool some of the people some of the time, but you cannot fool all the people all the time." People are usually on their best behavior while dating, especially toward the person they are trying to impress. Given enough time, we will see their true character in how they treat others.

You can also see how they handle stressful situations. Do they pray about major decisions? Do they pray about minor decisions? Do they pray for others when they have stressful situations? All of these are indicators of how they will likely act in the marriage.

Perhaps this is a good time to do your own self-evaluation of how you are handling stress, dealing with others, and serving God. Your future spouse (if they are Spirit-filled) may be observing you in the same way. We all have warts. We all have flaws. We are imperfect creatures. We have all sinned and fallen short of the glory of God (Rom. 3:23). Part of dating is to find out everything you can about the other person. We have to make a determination that we can tolerate those idiosyncrasies our potential spouse might have.

So while dating, take it seriously. I highly recommend finding a church group that offers many activities. This allows for you to observe the person you are dating while interacting with many people, and then you can validate their character. If you hit it off with them, you can further explore dating one on one until you develop a strong sense of who they are and their ability to meet the needs you have. I don't like to give a number when someone asks me how long they should date, but I will say that a healthy dating relationship takes about 12–18 months. That gives you time to see a person in action long enough to validate if they are consistent in their behavior of submission to God, love toward others, and ability to meet your specific needs

In my first marriage, my ex-wife was extremely insecure. She was easily upset by circumstances, and I didn't respond well to her need for understanding and compassion. Instead, I became frustrated and was dismissive of her feelings. Is it any wonder the relationship didn't last? We had an unplanned child together then rushed into marriage. Neither one of us had a strong relationship with God, and we really didn't know one another. As a result, we had a difficult time meeting the needs of one another. Less than 17 months after marriage, we were separated and eventually divorced.

The difference in my marriage to Cheri compared to my previous marriage is that I grew in my relationship with Christ, and Cheri grew in her relationship with Christ. As a result of yielding to the conviction of the Holy Spirit, we both became more selfless and more understanding of others. Cheri and I have always served in a ministry together and are better versions of ourselves as a couple than we are as individuals.

.

8

UNIFIED MARRIAGE

FAITH & TRUST IN A MARRIAGE

Faith and trust are so closely related that it's often hard to differentiate them. Hebrews 11:1 says:

Now faith is the substance of things hoped for, the evidence of things not seen

Faith has two components:

- Substance of things hoped for
- Evidence of things not seen

When we have faith in God, He shows himself to us, and he provides substance (something real, not imaginary), or the assurance of the things we hope for. God gives us evidence of things we can't see, like his presence. However, for that substance to come, for that evidence to be seen, we must step out or act on that faith:

James 2:14,17,24 — What doth it profit, my brethren, though a man say he hath faith, and have not works? can faith save him?... [17]Even so faith, <u>if it hath not works, is dead</u>, being alone...[24]Ye see then how that by works a man is justified, and not by faith only.

James tells us that if we do not act on our faith, then our faith "is dead." Dead faith means to have taken no action, and when you show no action, then you may have an unchanged life or a spiritually dead heart. If you have faith in God, you must act on that faith.

In my first marriage, I professed to have faith in God, but I didn't act on that faith. I wanted to go to church on Sundays, but I was easily swayed to not attend. If there was something I deemed more important, I would skip church. If I had a slight cold, I would skip church. If I was tired because I stayed up too late, I would skip church. If my ex-wife said she didn't feel like going, I would skip church. If I got into a fight with my ex-wife, I would skip church. I would never go to Sunday school or church on Wednesdays or Sunday nights either. Reading my Bible only happened when I was in church and the pastor asked me to stand and read from the Bible. My prayer life was inconsistent. Prayer was a way to petition God for something I wanted. It could be something material like a promotion, or it could be something more meaningful like peace in my marriage. I wouldn't talk to Jesus like a friend but more like a magic genie. I would ask for selfish things.

My infrequent church attendance resulted in an anemic spiritual life. I didn't pray, listen to God's word, go to church regularly, spend time with other Christians, or serve the Lord. Without these works, how could I hear God and obey what God wanted? Ultimately, I acted in the flesh. I was quick to get angry when things didn't go my way. I didn't treat my ex-wife with love and compassion, and in return, she was bitter and disrespectful toward me. The problem is, I knew the Word of God, but without prayer, meditation on God's Word, and good Christian accountability partners to discuss life's issues, I really didn't know what God wanted from me because I didn't tap into the power source He supplied, the Holy Spirit. How could I have acted on faith without knowing what God wanted for me? I was leading Eric; God wasn't leading Eric. I still wanted control of my own life. The result of Eric leading Eric was a miserable marriage and ultimately divorce because from the very start, God wasn't part of my life, let alone my marriage.

Faith
(acceptance)

Obedience
(acting)

Let me simplify this further. If I have faith in a chair to hold my weight but I have never tested that faith by sitting in the chair, some might argue that I really don't have faith. (I have a dead faith.) I would hope the chair holds my weight and might have faith in the mechanical engineer and manufacturing process, but unless I act upon that faith by finally sitting in the chair, I am not displaying my faith. To "act upon" means to obey. When I obey by sitting in the chair, I have the substance of what I hoped for (that the chair will hold me) and the evidence of things unseen (the manufacturing and engineering process I never witnessed firsthand).

Let's continue with the chair analogy. After I sit in the chair and discover it holds me, I have witnessed "good results." (The chair held me, and I didn't end up on the floor!) Now I can trust the chair. When those good results happen, I gain trust. Trust comes after the good results that are dependent upon our acceptance and obedience to God. Good results increase our faith and then allow us to have faith in more areas of our lives. If I start to tithe or serve in a church ministry and that results in more financially, then I have more trust in

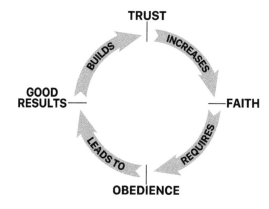

God. Based on that, I may now wish to put faith in God in another area of my life to find more good results. I may step out on faith and start trusting God by showing love toward my enemies and

forgiving them. That may result in a level of peace in my life I never thought possible! This cycle applied over and over is the key to Christian maturity. As we learn more about God and his promises, we will continue to put faith in him in more and more areas of our lives, thus producing good results.

Now let's apply this to our marriages. Managing a household has many responsibilities that are shared among husband and wife. When Cheri and I got married, we agreed that I would manage our finances, but she was very much involved! At first Cheri would remind me the first of the month was approaching; then she would sit next to me while I paid the bills. As you recall in the chapter on foundational needs, Cheri explained how she was the helicopter wife when it came to paying bills because of the financial struggles she faced with her ex. The bad results she had previously experienced made her lack faith in me to pay our bills. I'm not going to lie; at first this annoyed me. But she reminded me about her past, even though it wasn't I who caused the distrust. Now, after 13-plus years of marriage, the bills are paid on time, and we are no longer in any credit card or car debt. Cheri has complete trust in me regarding our finances. She doesn't remind me when bills are due or hover over my shoulder while I pay them. She just hands me the checkbook and receipts with a smile. The good results led to a trust regarding how I manage our finances. She trusts me so well that she jokes around with me often, saying she hopes God doesn't call me home before her because she wouldn't know how to pay the bills!

As we put faith in one another and produce good results, through the power of the Holy Spirit, we build trust in the marriage. To earn the trust of our spouse in all areas, we must continue to produce good results. The best way to ensure good results is for us to follow our authority, Jesus Christ—to follow the teachings of Jesus and to put faith in Christ and follow Him.

The Bible says in 1 Corinthians 11:3:

But I would have you know, that the head of every man is Christ; and the head of the woman is the man; and the head of Christ is God.

Christ is the head of all mankind. What does it mean to be the head? Simply put, it means "the first to lead." As our head or authority, we follow Christ's example by being obedient for our own good. Christ was obedient to God while here on Earth, and it benefited all of mankind.

Understanding this principle helps us to more easily follow the authorities in our lives because they are doing things in their role to help us. No matter who we are or what we do, we all have leaders and authorities that God has placed in our lives. Whether it's our bosses, the pastors at our churches, or a police officer, we all have authorities. In our marriages, both the husband and wife have roles that they fulfill. Who will manage the finances? Who will ensure kids do their homework? Who will do the cooking? Who will cut the grass? Some of these may be shared responsibilities, while it may be agreed that some will be the sole responsibility of one spouse. In 1 Corinthians 11:3, the Bible tells us that the husband is the spiritual leader in the home. He is to set the example of spiritual maturity in the home. He is to model Christ to his family, just like Christ modeled God to all of mankind.

In the construct of a biblical marriage, the woman is to respond to the spiritual leadership of her husband. In a healthy and godly marriage, it becomes natural for a woman to want to please and respond to Jesus Christ and a godly husband who follows Christ.

Wife: Spirit of the Home

Hello, ladies! This is Cheri. I told Eric that this portion of the book would be better received coming from a woman—a woman who has not always been a Christian, not always followed Jesus, and not always submitted to God or her husband. When I first became a Christian, which was just before Eric and I got married, I struggled with the words "wives shall submit." In my first marriage, when the minister met with us prior to the wedding, I remember asking him to eliminate the words "wives, submit to your husband" from our vows that he wanted me to repeat. Wow, and we wonder why that marriage ended?!

What I didn't realize in my first marriage, was there was no way I could have ever submitted because I didn't have a relationship with God. I knew *of* Him, had read the stories and believed, but I never read His Word, never talked to Him, never ever. Period. So the first thing we ladies need to do is to have our own personal relationship with God. As the "spirit of the home", we need to set the attitude of the home. I recommend setting the alarm a few minutes earlier than everyone else, and spending time with our Lord when the house is quiet. I know it's hard not to hit that snooze button, but you won't regret it. I know that I never regret taking the time to exercise, or taking the time and money to get my hair done. I always feel so good right after. Taking the time to get your heart right by reading God's Word and praying is *more* important than your hair, your makeup and your weight. It will make you feel good all day. Honestly, if you spend time with Jesus every day, you will glow from the inside, out!

So now that you've set your heart right, this submitting piece is a little eaiser. Submitting does not mean you are less than your husband. It does not mean you have a lesser value. If you look up the word in the dictionary, submit means to accept or yield to a governance or authority. Ephesians 5:22–25 says, "Husbands, love your wives," and "Wives, respect your husbands." Have you ever wondered why of all things in the Bible, God has to spell out clearly and succinctly that <u>husbands love</u> and <u>wives respect</u>?

> [22]*Wives submit yourselves unto your own husbands, as unto the Lord.*[23]*For the husband is the head of the wife, even as Christ is the head of the church: and he is the savior of the body....* [25]*Husbands, love your wives, even as Christ also loved the church, and gave himself for it.*

Well, ladies, if we were always loveable, then men would not have to hear God command them to love us. It would be easy for them to always love us. Face it; we can be a bit cranky sometimes, and the guys just don't realize all we have going on, do they? We have our monthly cycle that wreaks havoc on our bodies. Then, if it's God's will for us to give birth to a biological child, there is nine months of growing larger (and all the things associated with pregnancy) and then usually a year to lose the weight. (Of course, with me, it was close to three years. I figured I needed to stop saying I had "baby weight" at that point!) Oh, and don't forget that while we have all this baby making/baby rearing going on, we are faced with the whole beauty part of being a woman. We are cursed by the demons in our heads that tell us we aren't beautiful or that we're too fat. I'm only going to say this once, ladies: YOU ARE FEARFULLY AND WONDERFULLY MADE (Ps. 139:14)! So stop criticizing God's work. He doesn't like it when you do that.

Add to the body and baby thing the fact that we have our day jobs. Whether its inside the home or outside the home, we work hard! And whether your husband admits it or not, he knows it. Go away overnight one time, and leave the kids home with him—believe me; he'll get it.

Then the icing on the cake of being a woman is the lovely menopause. If you haven't reached that point yet, be warned, birthing babies is easier. I work out three to five times a week and have reduced my sugar and carb intake down to almost nothing, all just to maintain being 20 pounds overweight. My doctor recently told me to keep doing what I'm doing because I could gain more weight before this phase is over! (Remember, Cheri, you are fearfully and wonderfully made! SIGH!)

Like I said, we have a lot going on. So just breathe. Focus on the positive. Be grateful. Close your eyes and just thank God for all that he has blessed you with.

Now that you realize that it's not always easy for our husbands to love us, let's get back to that word we tend to cringe at: submission. Submission is not a statement of value. It doesn't mean I give up control. God designed men and women differently. We were designed to complement our spouse. Complement (with an E, not an I) means "to fill in," "to complete," "to make better," and "to bring to your perfection."

Remember, in Ephesians 5:21, God tells *all* of us (men and women) to "submit yourselves one to another in the fear of the Lord." It's not just about women submitting to men; it's about all of us submitting to God first. In verse 22, God says, "Wives submit yourselves unto your own husband, as unto the Lord." If our husbands are submitting themselves to Jesus Christ (accepting and yielding to him), then following our husbands should be just like following Christ. And don't you trust Christ?

Let's review the trust and faith figure. When Eric is walking close to God, reading the Bible, praying, serving, loving others, etc., I tend to see him more Christ-like, and that makes it easier to have faith in him and to obey his guidance (follow), which results in good things happening; this means I trust Eric! Unlike my last husband and the specific example of finances, I didn't trust my ex-husband to manage our debt, so I considered saving my own money so I could become self-reliant. My self-reliance grew distance between us.

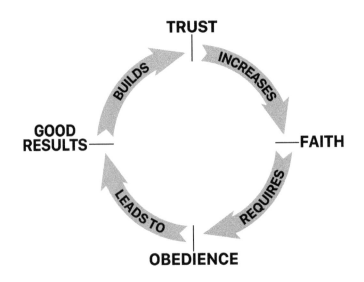

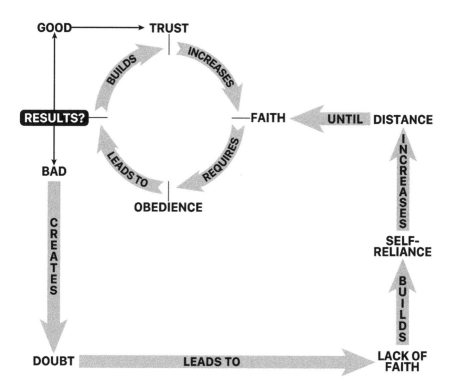

I didn't want to become self-reliant. I didn't want my marriage to end. As women, we naturally want our husbands to lead the family and to do well at their jobs. When the roles become reversed, it's uncomfortable and unnatural.

Ladies, maybe you are asking yourself, "How do I help my husband to be the leader God wants him to be?"

If your husband doesn't sense that he has encouragement and respect from you, he will lose the motivation to lead. Be encouraging, ladies. Don't talk down to your husband; that will only make things worse. Don't raise your voice and yell; he will tune you out. I know that when I get upset, my voice not only gets a lot louder but it goes up an entire octave. I have heard that voice on recordings, and I admit, it's annoying! I would tune me out too if I were him.

To respect means to admire, consider, recognize, honor, be kind to, uphold, and appreciate. Understand what feeds your husband's ability to lead. It starts with small, insignificant things. Let's say Eric suggests we eat hamburgers for dinner. Rather than dictate, "No! That's fattening! We're going to have fish," why not say, "Well, I already got fish out and thawed it. How about we do hamburgers tomorrow night?" Or if it really isn't a big deal and you can stick the fish back in the fridge, maybe you could say, "That's a good idea, easy and quick." Learn to choose your battles, and let him have influence on things that may be in your lane.

This may seem so elementary and minor, but this is how you can fuel your husband: by treating him and speaking to him in an encouraging and respectful way. Then, when faced with a big decision, your husband will seek you as a partner, and you will work together to decide the outcome. Be kinder to the man you are committing your heart to. It's that simple.

Husband: Loving Leader

I want to talk to you about the huge responsibility God has laid upon husbands to oversee the wife and children he has entrusted to you. As the husband, you are ultimately responsible for the behavior of those God has put into your care. Good thing God left husbands a roadmap—the Bible! The Bible is here to help husbands lead the way God wants them to lead as loving, spiritual, and humble leaders.

For a husband to grow the trust of his wife and family, he must be a humble servant who meets their needs. Servitude is the highest form of love and exemplifies Jesus:

1 Corinthians 16:14–16 – ¹⁴Let all your things be done with charity. ¹⁵I beseech you, brethren, (ye know the house of Stephanas, that it is the firstfruits of Achaia, and that they have addicted themselves to the ministry of the saints,)¹⁶ that ye submit yourselves unto such, and to every one that helpeth with us, and laboureth.

In verse 14, we see the word charity again. Charity is meeting the needs of others without expecting anything in return. Verse 15 tells us that we should be showing charity (ministering) to other saved Christians (saints). Our spouses should be the ones who are "helping us and laboring with us." This verse tells us to be servants to our spouses (our helpmeet) and to submit, or to think more highly of them and their needs than we do our own needs. When we do submit and serve the needs of our spouses, we are producing loving feelings and leading by example. Cheri has told me many times that it's easy for her to show respect and follow my lead when I am humbly serving the family and being Christ-like.

Husbands should show loving actions that will result in loving feelings and unity within the family. It's easy to understand but very hard to do apart from the Holy Spirit. You should be exemplifying Christ in your home. Your family will understand how God loves them by the way you love them.

Ephesians 5:23—25 – For the husband is the head of the wife, even as Christ is the head of the church: and he is the saviour of the body. [24]Therefore as the church is subject unto Christ, so let the wives be to their own husbands in every thing. [25]Husbands, love your wives, even as Christ also loved the church, and gave himself for it;

In order to emulate Jesus, we have to study him as a man and as God. We have to understand the Word of God, and we must pray to have Jesus fill our spiritual tanks. The closer to Jesus we are, the more loving we will be as leaders, the humbler and more sacrificial we will be, and the better our marriages will be.

Your authority is Jesus; therefore you need to be like him in order to be an example of him to your wife and children. As a loving leader, you must sacrifice yourself for those that follow you. Just like Christ sacrificed himself for the church, husbands need to sacrifice themselves for their wives.

My wife loves baseball and loves her home team, the Orioles. Personally, I'm not a big baseball fan. I'll root for our home team, but watching nine innings of baseball is not something that I like to do. Going to a game, getting a hot dog, and cheering on her team makes Cheri extremely happy. Because I love her so much, I'll sacrifice my personal time, my own desires, and about $100 to give her what she needs and desires. I wasn't so loving in my first marriage. I didn't sacrifice my time or money for my ex-wife. Spending time playing X-box or watching *SportsCenter* were more important to me than spending time alone with my ex-wife. My money was spent on my hobbies and interests, and very rarely did I spend money on her. These actions were fleshly and selfish and ultimately part of the reason our marriage failed.

When you show your wife she is loved by doing things for her, she will want to meet your needs as well. If you have children, you should lead by example. Loving fathers don't send their children out to weed the mulch bed without teaching them how to weed. It may seem odd, but by showing your kids how to do chores, they will also learn to observe you in other areas of life and the most important area: spirituality. When they see that you are willing to be the first to take action, to lead by example, and to serve those in your family, you are demonstrating loving leadership through servitude and humility.

Godly husbands and fathers are called to serve and be humble. Humility comes before unity. Sharing your fears and failures with your wife and children is another way to show your humility and dependence on God. No one is perfect, and it's okay to admit failure. Admitting failure shows your wife that you aren't perfect and that you need to rely on God to be Spirit-filled and Christ-like. When I admit to my wife that I failed, this brings us closer together.

Proverbs 16:19 – Better it is to be of an humble spirit with the lowly, than to divide the spoil with the proud.

The husband's job is to provide a hedge of protection around his family, just like God provides a hedge of protection around his people. If we properly follow God, we will be protected in spirit, mind, and body. A good Christian husband will properly protect his wife by providing loving spiritual leadership that provides protection of her spirit, mind, and body. This is God's management system for a marriage.

As we have already discussed, trust is built through good results. Good results come from being obedient followers of God through faith. If you aren't a good, loving leader and are disobedient to God, then bad results will happen, and your wife's trust in you will start to plummet. She will lose faith in you and will become self-reliant, distant, and potentially disrespectful.

With my ex-wife, I demanded respect and thought I deserved respect. Each time my ex-wife disrespected me, I would respond with a harsh tone and a more arrogant attitude and would act even less loving. I didn't feel the need to explain myself. It was a "because I said so" attitude. As Cheri mentioned, it's easier for a wife to let her husband lead if he is being a servant leader like Jesus Chris.

When Cheri and I argue, it's usually because she didn't show me the respect I wanted and I didn't react the right way either. As I've gotten more spiritually mature, I am now reacting better, and I've earned her respect. I act more loving (more Christ-like), and Cheri actually *likes* me. It's not rocket science.

When Cheri and I first got married, we had a new house built, and we mutually decided to save money by not building a deck right away. We decided that we would save our money and pay for that at a later time. Within the first two years of our marriage, Cheri's parents were celebrating their 50th wedding anniversary and wanted all their children and grandchildren to experience an Alaskan cruise with them. When I found out about the cruise, I told Cheri we could either build our deck or go to Alaska, but we really couldn't do both in the same year. She was understandably upset, and as the leader of our finances, I took the time to patiently explain to her why we could only afford one or the other. Once she understood, she easily followed my lead. Cheri also had a few ideas of how to save extra money and sell some things to allow us to do both things. I willingly listened to her and incorporated those ideas, and now the decision was both of ours. This was a huge contrast to my last marriage. I would have just said this is what we're doing—no explanation, no discussion—and if you don't like it, too bad.

I'm glad Christ was able to make me a new creature and that he equipped me with the power of the Holy Spirit. Praise the Lord! We each have roles to play in our marriages. When we take the time to explain ourselves lovingly, tapping into the Holy Spirit and acting like Jesus, it makes our difficult discussions much easier to follow.

Spiritual Leader

By walking closer to God, we can be strong spiritual leaders. The more we fill our own spiritual tanks, the easier it is to do. After we have prayed and read our Bibles, it becomes easier to follow this commandment from God:

> *Ephesians 5:25–27 – [25]Husbands, love your wives, even as Christ also loved the church, and gave himself for it; [26] That he might sanctify and cleanse it with the washing of water by the word, [27] That he might present it to himself a glorious church, not having spot, or wrinkle, or any such thing; but that it should be holy and without blemish.*

This passage tells us that we are supposed to sanctify and cleanse our wives by "washing her in the word." As our wives see us reading and praying, they will also start doing the same. Cheri has told me many times that she needs to see me reading my Bible at the kitchen table because it convicts her to do the same.

Another way to love your wife is to take the lead. Take the lead in praying with her, in making church a priority, and in leading a study of the Word of God (e.g., a Bible study); be a spiritual role model for Christ in the home. Men, you need to be faithful with your own Bible reading and faithful to church attendance to teach your wife and family what the Word of God says. Perhaps you don't feel you know the Bible well enough to interpret it; then seek out a godly mentor. Ask someone from your church to explain what the Bible says about a particular topic that maybe you or your family are struggling with. Don't guess if your family asks questions; seek godly wisdom from someone with more biblical knowledge. The husband as the spiritual leader will pray with his wife before major decisions, before bed at night, in times of crisis, and in times of praise. Leading by Jesus's example is pleasing to God and is exactly what he commands of a husband.

Observant Leader

Being observant is not a gift God gave me, so I personally struggle with this one. I work very hard to be aware of Cheri's needs:

1 Peter 3:7 – Likewise, ye husbands, dwell with them according to knowledge…

The best way to do this is to study your wife. Understand what your wife needs and wants, and give it to her. I like to read to fall asleep. I always have, and I probably always will. But my wife likes to wind down by talking for a few minutes before we shut the light off. Sometimes, if we find a good book that we both like, I'll read out loud to her. After we've talked or I've read out loud, we'll say a prayer together, and she will go to sleep while I turn on my book light and read. It wasn't always like this, because I didn't observe her in her bedtime routine. In the beginning of our marriage, I noticed how restless she was when she was trying to fall asleep, and I would get annoyed because it would disrupt my reading. One night, instead of picking up my book, I decided to talk to her about the day and about what she had going on the next day. We snuggled together while we talked and both really enjoyed that connection. I noticed that she slept more soundly that night. I realized she was restless when she didn't unwind from the pressures of the day. She needed that time with me, as the spiritual leader, before bed to help her unwind.

Set aside time to talk to your wife about her needs and spending quality time with her. Discuss what's on her mind and in her heart. When you connect with your wife this way, it shows her how much you love and cherish her by meeting that need.

Protector

Ephesians 5:25 – Husbands, love your wives, even as Christ also loved the church, and gave himself for it;

1 Peter 3:7 – ...giving honour unto the wife, as unto the weaker vessel...

As spiritual leaders in our homes, we are supposed to protect our wives in mind, body, and spirit. We should be protecting them from harm. In addition to physical harm, we should set up a hedge of protection around them to protect them from worldly influences. At home, I'm very cautious about what I allow my family to watch on TV, what I allow them to hear on the radio, whom they spend time with, and other sinful things of this world the devil uses to tear down the wife's spirit. A wife will feel loved when the husband takes loving actions to protect her.

In addition to the example above, there are a few specific roles the husband needs to play as the protector of his wife:

1. The He-Man
The Bible states that God made women as weaker vessels. It is not talking about weak in spirit; it truly means physically weaker. Biologically, men have 20% more red blood cells than women do. The red blood cells have hemoglobin that carries oxygen through the blood stream. Oxygen is used by the muscles to burn calories and create fuel and energy for the body. Since men have 20% more red blood cells, we typically will not get as physically tired as quickly as women. Therefore, a man doing the same exact work for the same amount of time as a woman will not be as tired.

When my wife and I have worked all day and we both come home exhausted, it should be my job to take on the extra load of household chores. I have more energy than she does, so if there are dishes to be done, I should do them. Guys, I get it. You are tired too. But this is when you will make God happy. This is how you will make your wife happy. When the Bible says to give "honor to the weaker vessel," it means to take on the physical burden.

As husbands, if we recognize this biblical and biological truth, we can prevent our wives' physical exhaustion; in return, they will appreciate how we are taking care of them, and it will make them feel closer to us.

2. The Security Guard

We are also called to be the protectors of the family. We need to be observant of our surroundings. We need to make sure we are looking for signs of danger that may threaten our wives and families' safety. I would jump in front of a bullet for Cheri, so why would I drop her off on the corner of downtown Baltimore and say, "Okay, have fun. Stay safe"? I would instead escort her to make sure she gets to where she needs to be safely.

My wife has an odd fear of frogs. Yes, frogs, and yes, she knows it's odd to be afraid of something that can't harm her, but it is what it is. I've known this about her since before we were even dating. Everyone makes fun of her, and she has learned to take it well, but this is a very real phobia that she has, and I will protect her. I know that in the humid summers in the suburbs of Baltimore, frogs are prevalent, so I am always looking for them. When my wife and I come home at night, I pull the car into the garage and close the door. Before she gets out of the car, I'm looking for those things that make her uncomfortable or threaten her safety, and then I reassure her that it's safe. If I ever forget and walk in the house before checking for her "little enemies," she feels unsafe and unloved and not very close to me.

The concept of opening doors for ladies is for that very purpose. It's not just what people refer to as chivalry. Opening the door for my wife shows respect, but it also says, "I've looked around the area, and it is safe and secure." When we open the door for our wives, it is telling our wives that we love them and care for them and their safety.

3. The Garbage Collector
Husbands should be doing the dirty jobs, anything that's a potential hazard. Taking out trash isn't just about her not wanting to get dirty; it is you braving the potential illness for her.

We may not be in danger of getting ill from taking out the trash, but not that long ago, trash removal was about removing decomposing carcasses. When we volunteer to do things like change the oil, put air in the tires, dig in the garden, or remove trash, we show our wives that we are willing to take the risk rather than them.

Peacemaker

Jesus was always looking for peaceful resolutions to conflict. Remember when the soldiers were coming to take Jesus away and Peter cut off the ear of one of them? Jesus told Peter in John 18:11, "Put up thy sword into the sheath." Jesus was telling Peter to put away his weapon and not to fight. As spiritual leaders, we need to look for opportunities to bring peace into the marriage. We have three critical tasks to make the marriage more peaceful: We should value our wives' opinions, use loving words, and end the arguing in our homes. These are all unifying functions we play as the husband. As the leaders in the home, it is our job to keep the marriage functioning in a healthy, unified way.

1. Value Her Opinion
The roles of husbands and wives may be different as they support the marriage, but just because the husband is the spiritual leader, this doesn't mean he is more important.

1 Peter 3:7 – ...as being heirs together of the grace of life...

We need to validate that our wives' opinions matter! A good leader will lead with the input of those he serves. Our wives want to know that their input is heard and respected, and it's the husband's job to make the wife and children feel safe to express their opinions. God made men and women different on purpose. Men are typically logical by nature, while women are cautious and caring. We become members of a team once we are married, and we complement one another. To have healthy marriages, we must embrace these different strengths and viewpoints by respecting what each of us brings into the marriage.

Asking your wife for her opinion makes her feel closer to you. Know, cherish, and love your wife by respecting, valuing, and contemplating her advice and opinions. If your wife is afraid to share her viewpoint, the marriage is unhealthy. As a husband, you need to take time to consult with your wife regarding day-to-day decisions and value her input; otherwise, she may fear she doesn't have a say and that she has no free will. A loving leader will recognize this fear and be sure to include their wife in the decision-making process.

God wired men and women to see things differently. By expressing our opinions to our wives, we can use their valuable input to be better leaders. I remember there were times when I would downplay my wife's need for comfort or safety. I remember we went to the beach one year, and I told her it was silly to put on sunscreen since we'd only be out for a few hours. That's not the action of a loving leader. Lo and behold, I got sunburned!

We once took a 17-hour road trip from Baltimore to Memphis. I decided we would get up early and drive all day. To prepare for the trip, I checked the oil and the tire pressure, cleaned the windows, reviewed maps to plot out ideal gas spots, checked for the shortest route, etc. Meanwhile, my wife was packing pillows, water, and snacks and lunches while also making sure the boys had enough things to keep them busy. I remember telling her we didn't have room for those pillows and that the food would just be under our feet and in the way. Well, about six hours into the trip, everyone really appreciated those pillows and those snacks. The pillows made the boys more comfortable, and the snacks reduced the number of times we had to stop for food (plus saved us money!). You see, as a team of diverse perspectives, we made the trip both efficient and comfortable. To this day, I never question my wife when it comes to our comfort.

Over the years, I've learned to value my wife's perspective. If what your wife requests doesn't dishonor God or hurt anyone, then just put on some sunscreen or let her pack the water and food for the car trip. You may think it's silly and unnecessary, but it tells your wife, "I love and respect you." Not doing it, or pushing back, undermines her trust and respect for you, especially if the bad results she fears come true. She may view you as acting a bit reckless, and she may think you are undeserving of her loyalty.

2. Loving Words

We all need to choose our words carefully. Proverbs 18:21 says, "Death and life are in the power of the tongue." A husband must lead by example and should communicate his love toward his wife by the words he uses:

> *Proverbs 16:24 – Pleasant words are as an honeycomb, sweet to the soul, and health to the bones.*

Loving and encouraging words build your wife's spirit and bring her health:

> *1 Peter 3:8 – Finally, be ye all of one mind, having compassion one of another, love as brethren, be pitiful, be courteous:*

In a marriage, we need to take care of each other. Being "pitiful" means to consider others first, to have compassion, and to be courteous (no slander, no putdowns, no arguing, no backbiting, and no negative words):

> *Ephesians 4:25–27 – ²⁵Wherefore putting away lying, speak every man truth with his neighbour: for we are members one of*

another. ²⁶Be ye angry, and sin not: let not the sun go down upon your wrath: ²⁷Neither give place to the devil.

Remember, you are the image of Christ to your wife, and you need to make sure you are using loving words, thus giving your wife "health to the bones" (Prov. 16:24). As part of God's commandments, we need to love our wives as Christ loves the church (Eph. 5:25). Christ is God, and God is love. God is incapable of ill will. When you show your wife ill will by arguing, putting her down, using negative words, then you are crushing her spirit. As her husband, you need to use loving words to give health to your wife and health to your marriage.

Connecting to your wife is more than physically connecting to your wife. Your wife wants to connect to you through words. Your wife wants to talk to you. My wife loves to share her day with me after work because I am her best friend. You should be your wife's best friend too. Women feel connected to us through conversation. In our home, there are three times a day that I make sure to connect with my wife: when I get home from work, when we eat dinner together, and before we go to sleep at night. During those connecting moments, she just wants me to listen to her, to listen to her thoughts, and to find out how her day was, and she wants me to tell her about my day. When I connect through conversation, she knows I care.

3. Stop the Arguing

We all have disagreements in any relationship, especially in our marriages. Typically, as we fight, our human nature will elevate the tension. It is only through a meek spirit that we can disarm the other person. Just as love creates love, bitterness can create hate. When we get hurt, we want to retaliate. However, the Bible tells us a different approach:

1 Peter 3:9 – Not rendering evil for evil, or railing for railing: but contrariwise blessing; knowing that ye are thereunto called, that ye should inherit a blessing.

Someone has to stop the cycle when arguments are escalating and when hurtful things were said. It is the husband's job in a marriage to do that. Proverbs tells us how:

Proverbs 15:1 – A soft answer turneth away wrath: but grievous words stir up anger.

When we refrain our tongue and when we stop the arguing by retaliating with a soft answer rather than hurtful words, we can bring the argument to an end.

One day just before work, my wife and I had an argument. It was minor, but we both left for work in a huff. I went to work, threw myself into meetings, and soon forgot about the argument. On the other hand, my wife had a bad day. Her emails were bitter, she was angry toward her coworkers, and she was not very productive throughout the day. She didn't realize it at the time, but our argument had negatively affected her in everything she did. When I got home and noticed she was still angry, it then dawned on me: "Oh yeah, we had a fight this morning."

While I was able to focus on work, throw my mind into the task at hand, and not even remember we were fighting, she had been affected by the fight the entire day. She found it hard to concentrate and focus until the argument had been resolved.

In 1 Peter 3:9, God commands us to end the argument. I have learned over the years that when my wife appears to be "picking a fight" with me, she isn't doing it to nag or complain. She is actually doing it because there is conflict or an offense that she needs to get resolved. As men, when we are acting as peacemakers, we need to sit down and talk to our wives about what is bothering them. If we don't try to stop the argument, we are actually making it worse. As peacemakers, it is our job to unite with our wives. That is why God calls us to stop the argument.

4. Truth in Love

A final way men unify the family by playing the role of peacemaker is by being honest and transparent:

1 Peter 3:10 – For he that will love life, and see good days, let him refrain his tongue from evil, and his lips that they speak no guile:

The meaning of guile is craftiness, sneaky, facade, betrayal, deceit. We need to communicate with loving words and refrain from evil: "speak no guile." Men, we need to be creating unity with our words to help create joy-filled homes in order to have good days. In addition to being honest in how we speak, husbands should conduct their lives honestly.

We should lead by example, just like Christ did when he was here. He gave us an example: We are to conduct ourselves with integrity. We spoke about trust in the chapter on relational needs. How can you build trust and faith with your wife if you are giving her reasons to not trust you? Are you cheating on taxes? Are you stealing little things from the office? Are you barely working your eight-hour shift but claiming you worked eight hours? Are you telling your kids to pretend they are younger than they really are to get $2 off a movie ticket? Is your integrity worth $2? Your wife's trust leads to faith in you as a leader and helps her to follow you in obedience. By lying, using guile, we can exchange that trust to save a few dollars at the movies. She can see it and your kids can see it, and it undermines your leadership.

RESULTS OF GOOD LEADERSHIP

If we act in the role of loving leader, God promises good results in our marriages. Those good results are a happy life, answered prayers, and a holy family:

Ephesians 5:25–27 – Husbands, love your wives, even as Christ also loved the church, and gave himself for it; ^{26} That he might sanctify and cleanse it with the washing of water by the word, ^{27} That he might present it to himself a glorious church, not having spot, or wrinkle, or any such thing; but that it <u>should be holy and without blemish</u>.

Your wife will be the godly wife God wants her to be if you are leading her the way you should be. Your wife and children are a measure of your righteousness. Ephesians 5:27 tell us the results of the sanctification of your wife's holiness is a reflection of your loving spiritual leadership in the home. The more you emulate Christ, the holier your wife will be.

I remember years ago, after Cheri and I were married, she looked at our pastor's wife and said to me, "I wish I was more like her." I remember thinking at the time, *I wish you acted more like her too.* What a judgmental thing to think! What I didn't realize was that my wife's holiness is a reflection of how well I am leading her spiritually. The reason she didn't act like the pastor's wife is because I didn't act like a pastor. I wasn't being a good Christian. I wasn't faithful to my Bible reading, prayer time, or church attendance. Husbands, it is our job to wash our wives in the word so that they can be "holy and without blemish." I now know that this is *my* responsibility.

Men, our wives will act holy if we put an emphasis on Christ in our homes. If we are doing our job as loving spiritual leaders by meeting our wives' needs biblically and by leading by example, our wives will reflect back to us the example we set. Ephesians 5:27 says our church (i.e., our wives) will be without spot or wrinkle and blameless but only if we sanctify them. How do you sanctify? Wash your wife in the word, be righteous, pray, and read the Bible together.

Ephesians 5:28 – So ought men to love their wives as their own bodies. He that loveth his wife loveth himself.

We saw earlier, in Genesis, that the Bible says we are one flesh. This passage refers to us as one body. Our brain tells the body to eat (nourish), to wash (cleanse), and to meet the needs of the body. Why? So that it functions properly. Meeting the needs of our own bodies and having good nourishment leads to an easier existence. Men are the head of the body, and they should be the ones to nourish and cleanse that body spiritually.

If you are about to say, "I do," or when you said, "I do," you entered into a covenant, not a contract—a covenant. You are committing to God that you will train and teach, nourish and care for, lead by example, and sacrifice for her. A contract is a two-way transaction and is based on conditional clauses that explain how two entities will conduct business together. It also creates conditions under which there are consequences for breaking one person's part of the agreement and ways for people to terminate the contract. Basically, if you do *this*, I will do *that*. It also has clauses in which either party can get out of doing things. A covenant is UNCONDITIONAL. No matter what your wife does or doesn't do, you are committed to doing your part. It's not optional. Remember, agape love is not based on expectations. I cannot base my love or my actions on expectations of my wife doing her part or the relationship will fall apart.

Abundant Life

Ephesians 5:28–30 – So ought men to love their wives as their own bodies. He that loveth his wife loveth himself. ²⁹ For no man ever yet hated his own flesh; but nourisheth and cherisheth it, even as the Lord the church: ³⁰ For we are members of his body, of his flesh, and of his bones.

A loving spiritual leader is the one that stops the arguing and doesn't stir up strife but builds up and edifies. He is the one that can take a contentious tone and turn away wrath.

1 Peter 3:10–11 – For he that will love life, and see good days, let him refrain his tongue from evil, and his lips that they speak no guile: ¹¹Let him eschew evil, and do good; let him seek peace, and ensue it.

A husband must eschew evil (to avoid habitually, especially on moral or practical grounds; shun). If you are cheating, lying, not sharing the whole story, stealing, or using harsh words, you are not seeking peace. If you are making peace by seeking to understand

and meet the needs of others at your own expense, then you will earn the respect, the trust, and the faith of your wife. In a nut-shell, following Jesus by being Christ-like in the home will result in abundant life (John 10:10) and good days (1 Peter 3:10). When you are married, you are one flesh, so when you meet your wife's needs, you are also meeting your own needs. When you cherish your wife by paying her compliments, alone or in front of others, you are making your life more abundant. When you nourish your wife by turning off the TV to spend time connecting with her, you are making <u>good days</u>.

> *John 10:10 – I am come that they might have life, and that they might have it more abundantly.*

Let me explain the abundant life idea better. Ever play a sport when you were tired? Did you enjoy it? You might have run in the race, but it wasn't an abundant amount of fun, was it? About 10 years ago, my wife and I walked in a three-day breast cancer walk. It was a total of 60 miles in three days! Walking 60 miles takes a lot of time to prepare for. Unfortunately, I did not take it very seriously, and I didn't train like I should have. I figured if I could run two miles on a treadmill, I could certainly walk 20 miles in one day, no problem! Boy, was I wrong. The first night I passed out after the first 20 miles while waiting in line for the showers. Day two, I had a blistered and calloused left foot that was so bad I couldn't even finish that day. Each night the campsite had concerts and celebrations for the walkers, and I didn't even get to participate. Yes, I completed the event, but it wasn't very fun for me or my wife.

The next year we did the same walk again. This time we spent many months preparing our bodies for the walk, and I completed the entire 60-mile walk. I had the energy to participate in the evening activities, and my wife and I met really good friends on the trip. We had a great time. It was the same exact activity, but we had more fun; it was more abundant. That is what this verse means: You can have life and have it more abundantly.

Some people go through marriage that is abundant, while others have a daily struggle. When you nourish, cherish, and prepare your marriage, you will enjoy your marriage more, and you will have abundant joy and good days. The result of treating your wife properly by meeting her needs will result in an abundant marriage that thrives!

Answered Prayer

Finally, not only will following Christ give you abundant life and good days but it will allow your prayers to be answered:

> *1 Peter 3:7 – Likewise, ye husbands, dwell with them according to knowledge, giving honour unto the wife, as unto the weaker vessel, and as being heirs together of the grace of life; that your prayers be not hindered.*

> *1 Peter 3:12 – For the eyes of the Lord are over the righteous, and his ears are open unto their prayers: but the face of the Lord is against them that do evil.*

God will not answer the prayers of those that disobey. If we aren't treating our wives properly, then our prayers become hindered. This was so important that God said it twice: once in verse 7 and again in verse 12.

If you treat your wife right, the result is "good days" and "abundant life," but if you treat your wife poorly, if you live unrighteous, then you will have your prayers hindered. After all, how do you expect your wife to respect you as a spiritual leader if you are unrighteous? How can she put her faith in you when you aren't putting your faith in the Lord? Husbands must meet the high standards in their marriage to live a righteous life all the time, putting the needs of others first over their own needs.

Epilogue

The top three reasons for divorce, according to an August 2013 survey done by Institute for Divorce Financial Analysts are below:

- 22% – Financial issues
- 28% – Infidelity
- 43% – Incompatibility

These issues relate to needs that were outlined throughout the chapters in the book. Let's look at what we have learned so far and see how loving actions produce loving feelings to create unity in our marriages.

Financial Issues

Financial issues were discussed in the chapter on foundational needs. We all have the need for safety, shelter, food, etc. These needs are provided by paying our rent and our utilities (e.g., electricity and water) and by buying groceries. If we don't have the finances to afford those things, a need is not being met. Also, if one of the spouses in a marriage spends all the money or controls the money to a point where those things are threatened, a need is not being met. When most couples fight over money, it is typically caused by one person living beyond their means and the other one feeling threatened. This leaves the threatened person feeling as if their spouse doesn't love them, because they are not providing those basic essentials, and therefore divorce can result.

INFIDELITY

Infidelity issues were discussed in the chapter describing relational needs. As we discussed earlier, when two people fall in love, it is the result of people meeting each other's needs. Infidelity starts in the mind and heart way before any actions are taken. Our needs exist no matter if we are married or not. If our spouses stop meeting our needs, then we are tempted to find others that will meet those needs.

When our spouses do not meet our needs sexually or emotionally, we are tempted to look for others to meet those expectations.

INCOMPATIBILITY

I saved incompatibility for last because it is a catchall phrase that really indicates one person stopped meeting the needs of the spouse and vice versa. As we indicated in the infidelity section, when needs are not met within the marriage, we look for those needs to be met outside the marriage. We may not cross the line to infidelity, but when we look to others to meet the needs our spouses are not meeting, sooner or later we will be convinced we just aren't compatible and will move on to something "better."

Incompatibility is basically two people that were meeting each other's needs and just stopped doing it. There may not ever be infidelity, but they could become two people who live in the same home, raise the children, and coexist. Eventually they will choose to move on. We really don't need to find a new person; we just need to get back to the place where we try harder to meet our spouses' needs.

This book is the result of decades of worldly decisions combined with years of biblical research and the knowledge gained through a variety of sermons from a multitude of pastors. It is our hope that our life lessons combined with biblical truth will help you avoid the mistakes we've made and have a better understanding of the love–need connection, which will lead to a joy-filled and resilient marriage. If you make God a priority in your marriage, God will bless it!

CPSIA information can be obtained
at www.ICGtesting.com
Printed in the USA
FFHW02n2234091018

9 781732 683334